BAD APPLES

BAD APPLES

HOW TO MANAGE DIFFICULT EMPLOYEES, ENCOURAGE GOOD ONES TO STAY, AND BOOST PRODUCTIVITY

BRETTE MCWHORTER SEMBER AND **TERRENCE J. SEMBER**
FOREWORD BY **ROSANNE T. DEE**

AVON, MASSACHUSETTS

Published by Adams Business,
an imprint of Adams Media, a division of F+W Media, Inc.
57 Littlefield Street, Avon, MA 02322. U.S.A.
www.adamsmedia.com

ISBN 10: 1-60550-004-6
ISBN 13: 978-1-60550-004-1

Printed in the United States of America.

J I H G F E D C B A

Library of Congress Cataloging-in-Publication Data
is available from the publisher.

This publication is designed to provide accurate and authoritative information with regard to the subject matter covered. It is sold with the understanding that the publisher is not engaged in rendering legal, accounting, or other professional advice. If legal advice or other expert assistance is required, the services of a competent professional person should be sought.

—From a *Declaration of Principles* jointly adopted by a Committee of the American Bar Association and a Committee of Publishers and Associations

Many of the designations used by manufacturers and sellers to distinguish their product are claimed as trademarks. Where those designations appear in this book and Adams Media was aware of a trademark claim, the designations have been printed with initial capital letters.

This book is available at quantity discounts for bulk purchases.
For information, please call 1-800-289-0963.

ACKNOWLEDGMENTS

Our thanks to the many employees we have managed over the years, as well as the managers we have learned from. Many thanks go to our superb agent, Gina Panettieri, for her incredible vision and faith in all of her authors. This book would be sorely lacking were it not for the input of Michael Devlin of Berchem Moses & Devlin in Milford, Connecticut, who lent his employment law expertise. Chelsea King and the entire team at Adams Media have been with us all the way through this project and have been wonderful to work with. Love and thanks to our children, Quinne and Zayne, who would walk by the office and roll their eyes because Mom and Dad were working on "the book" *again*.

CONTENTS

FOREWORD | xi

INTRODUCTION | xiii

PART 1
ABOUT **BAD** APPLES | 1

CHAPTER 1 | 3
WHAT IS A BAD APPLE?

CHAPTER 2 | 19
TYPES OF BAD APPLES

CHAPTER 3 | 41
BAD APPLES YOU INHERIT

CHAPTER 4 | 55
BAD APPLES OUTSIDE OF YOUR CONTROL

PART 2

PROBLEM-**SOLVING** TECHNIQUES | 71

CHAPTER 5 | 73
MOTIVATING BAD APPLES TO BECOME GOOD

CHAPTER 6 | 91
MAINTAINING GOOD APPLES

CHAPTER 7 | 115
DEALING WITH PERSONALITY CONFLICTS

CHAPTER 8 | 133
CULTIVATING CONFLICT RESOLUTION SKILLS

CHAPTER 9 | 149
DISCIPLINING BAD APPLES

CHAPTER 10 | 159
DITCHING BAD APPLES

CHAPTER 11 | 175
CONSIDERING LEGAL RAMIFICATIONS

PART 3
FEND OFF FUTURE **BAD** APPLES | 187

CHAPTER 12 | 189
CREATE A POSITIVE WORK ENVIRONMENT

CHAPTER 13 | 207
AVOID HIRING BAD APPLES

CONCLUSION | 225
BALANCING THE APPLE CART

INDEX | 235

FOREWORD

In today's business environment, where every word is evaluated to ensure political correctness, it was refreshing to read a book that offers sound, practical advice to help you deal with the bad apples in your organization. This book is a must-read for any manager, and it's probably a majority of leaders, who has ever had to deal with a bad apple.

As a business consultant, I encounter bad apple behavior in all forms as I help employers and leaders deal with the inevitable fallout. This fallout can be made much easier if you follow the advice of the authors, who offer solutions that blend development and discipline. They point out that the most important test for determining if you have a bad apple is whether or not the person is having a negative impact on the bottom line. They also explain the various types of bad apple behaviors and offer suggestions on how to evaluate whether the source of negative behavior is the person, the environment, or the team. As managers invest a tremendous amount of time and energy in dealing with the issue of bad apple behavior, this book guides them to determine whether they are making a good or bad investment. One bad apple can truly destroy teamwork and morale and, if the leader is reluctant to address the issues, it also can destroy trust in the leader. The authors point out the need for managers to stay in touch with their teams so that they can identify negative behavior early in the game, because some employees show one persona to the boss and treat their peers much differently. If a manager is looking and paying attention to team dynamics he or she may spot a problem before it gets out of control. Suggestions on establishing norms for the team, skill building, and appropriate training are also discussed.

Conflict resolution is one of the key communication skills for leaders, so I would recommend this book to all managers. I would also offer it as a preread to any of the conflict resolution workshops I conduct for leaders. Very specific techniques are spelled out that can serve as a guide to managers.

The importance of identifying the types of people you want to hire and having an effective recruiting and screening process will prevent the hiring of new bad apples. Making sure you make smart hiring decisions will prevent problems that sap energy from the organization. Remember, the leader's responsibility in motivating and directing his or her team sends a message that he or she takes the issue of team behavior seriously. Being clear on expectations is another important aspect of managing behavior.

Finally, the authors' upbeat and positive position that it is the leaders' responsibility to create a work environment where people can grow and develop communicates an inherent belief that managers control their outcomes. The importance of developing solid, trusting relationships with your people will help determine if an employee will turn into a bad apple.

I love the no-nonsense, take-accountability tone of this book and have learned many new ideas to use in my own business consulting.

Rosanne Dee
Owner of RT Dee and Associates,
a human resource consulting and training firm
August 18, 2008

INTRODUCTION

If management was just about making smart business decisions and being knowledgeable in the industry, many more managers would be successful. However, management is more about people smarts and understanding how to work with, influence, and direct the people who work for you. A large part of people management is learning how to manage bad apples.

A bad apple is one of those employees who is just plain trouble or completely annoying. While it's likely that most of your employees do a good job and are reasonably easy to work with, you will, from time to time, come upon someone who is difficult. Bad apples on your team can include anyone from the woman who constantly puts down other people on the team, the guy who is never on time for anything, the woman with the chip on her shoulder, to the man who simply will not stop talking about women's bodies. Occasionally in your career you may have to deal with bad apples with even worse qualities—someone who steals from the company or undermines you to your boss. Fortunately these instances are rare. But, in short, a bad apple is the person on your team who makes your life, or those of your other employees, difficult.

If you've got a bad employee, you may think, "Fire him!" Certainly that's a solution some of the time, but there are a lot of situations in which that isn't possible—he's the boss's nephew, she is best friends with your company's best client, he's the only one who knows how to navigate a software program your company is stuck with, or there just aren't any good replacements available.

In these kinds of situations, you need to learn how to cope with, control, influence, and sometimes work around your bad apple. You also need to know how to keep one horrendous employee from souring your entire team. It may sound like an impossible task, but there are strategies you can employ to keep one bad apple from spoiling the whole bunch.

This book is the answer to all of your conundrums in these situations. We've put together everything you need to know about working with a bad apple, and practical solutions to the problems you face when you're managing an employee who is difficult. Whether you want (or need) to work around the difficult employee, rehabilitate him, fire him, suspend him, reduce his influence on your team, or learn techniques for keeping your sanity when dealing with a bad apple, we have the solutions you need.

PART 1

ABOUT
BAD APPLES

CHAPTER 1

WHAT IS A BAD APPLE?

We've all worked with employees who weren't always the best and the brightest, but a bad apple is someone who is especially difficult, troublesome, or hard to work with. Before you were a manager, working with these kinds of people made your life hard, but now you have to manage, control, motivate, and guide that person for the benefit of your company—and deal with any fallout that person causes within your team. This can be challenging for even the most experienced manager, but there are definitely ways to do so without losing your sanity. A bad apple doesn't have to mean that your team or professional future is down the drain.

ch 1. What Is a Bad Apple?

ch 2. Types of Bad Apples

ch 3. Bad Apples You Inherit

ch 4. Bad Apples Outside of Your Control

BEHAVIOR

To understand what a bad apple is, you need to recognize the basic types of behavior that make a bad employee. There is no one picture of what a bad apple is. These types of workers come with a variety of traits, personalities, and problems. Some are so easy to spot that they may as well have flashing lights on their heads. Things like tardiness, leaving work early, failing to follow instructions, rudeness, argumentativeness, and inability to take direction are obvious indicators that you have a problem on your hands. You won't feel confident that these employees can adequately do the job, fulfill a task, or be trusted when you need to count on them. Everyone else on your team will also dislike the person, or know that she is trouble.

There are also bad apples who are more difficult to identify because they try to make a good impression on you personally, but make the lives of their coworkers miserable when you're not there. In these situations, you have to read the signs from the others around them. At meetings, do eyes roll when the questionable employee makes a comment? Does she always volunteer when you ask for something to be done, but doesn't step up when others ask for help? Are there rumblings among your team members about her work quality, work ethic, or personality? An employee who puts up a good front for you, but makes your team members miserable, is just as dangerous for your team and company as the employee who is obviously bad.

Some undesirable employees can be identified because of the situations they put you in. Compare the everyday, nondisability-related accommodations you are making for one particular employee to those you make for others. If you find that you always have to readjust project deadlines for Tom, or Julie always requests that a sketch be redrawn to make it easier for her to work on, you've got a bad apple.

The simplest and best way to identify a bad employee is to determine if he negatively affects the company's bottom line. This is, after all, the most important test of an employee. If whatever he is or isn't doing makes it harder for others to get their work done, or for him to complete his, the bottom line will reflect it. The ultimate outcome of his attitude or behavior is that the company is not performing as well as it could.

PERFORMANCE AND PRODUCTIVITY

One of the biggest responsibilities of being a manager is ensuring that all of your employees positively contribute to the company. No business can afford employees who do not have a positive impact on the bottom line. Anyone who causes decreased revenue or increased cost is a problem for both you and the company and you should pay close attention to this bad apple. If your team or department is not producing as expected—or is not showing increased growth at the rate you hoped—you should carefully consider the role that one bad employee is playing in the big picture.

It's one thing to say that a person has a negative impact on productivity, but it is another to actually show that this is the case. Measuring a person's productivity is very industry- and job-specific—but here are a few guidelines you can rely on:

- Evaluate the volume and quality of the work that person produces
- Look at billable hours if the employee has an impact on them

- Compare the employee's productivity with other employees who do similar work in your company
- Make note of employees who produce the right quantity of work, but do not meet the levels of quality they should be achieving
- Determine if the employee is always seeking to improve on the work he puts out
- Notice whether the employee fulfills your company's standard operating procedures

You should look not only at that employee's personal productivity, but also at how he influences productivity for the entire team or company. An employee who does not do his job well is an obvious problem, but one who drags down the work of others is just as dangerous—but harder to spot because the drain on the company may be subtle and quiet.

apples to apples A CASE STUDY

Michael and Jenna are both sales associates for a siding company. They were both hired at the same time, but Michael had a little more experience writing proposals. Once Jenna learned this, she came to him with almost every single proposal she wrote, asking for his help and input. Michael was happy to help at first, but Jenna eventually took up so much of his time that he had trouble keeping up with his own work. While he tried to get her to learn from the advice he'd given in the past, Jenna always seemed to have a reason she needed his help. While Michael was able to meet his deadlines and sell successfully, the drain Jenna created on Michael's productivity prevented him from achieving the level of success he was capable of—and that the company needed. Fortunately, their manager, Jackie, was very in tune with her team and asked Jenna how often she went to Michael for help. Her answer was vague, so Jackie talked to Michael and learned what had been going on. She told Michael that if Jenna needed help, to send her to Jackie's office. At first Jenna was reluctant to ask Jackie for help, but, with Jackie's guidance, she soon learned how to successfully write her own proposals. Meanwhile, Michael was able to focus and increased his selling levels.

REASONS FOR BAD APPLE BEHAVIOR

Just as there are a lot of employee behaviors that are problematic, there are many reasons that can explain the behavior. If you can pinpoint and understand the reasons behind your employee's actions (or inactions), you'll be in a better position to solve the problem that is causing the behavior.

Some common reasons for below par activity include:

- He doesn't like his job
- He doesn't like the work environment
- She doesn't like her coworkers
- He feels dissatisfied within the company
- She has skill set deficiencies that she is trying to manage or cover up
- He really has no idea he's not measuring up
- She is experiencing a personal, health, or family problem outside of work
- He has a clash with management
- He has basic personality traits that are incompatible with the job or company

The best way to find out the reason behind your employee's behavior is to talk to her. Find out what her concerns are, how she feels, and what's going on in her life. It's impossible to properly correct something if you can't identify the cause, and sometimes managers tend to overthink things when there's a simple explanation. If you have an employee who is not turning in projects on time, you could extrapolate all sorts of complicated reasons for this—she can't work with the new version of the software, she's trying to make you look bad, etc.—when the explanation may be as simple as the fact that another manager is giving her work that is more urgent. Remember, you need to find the root of the problem before you can fix it.

Unless you understand the underlying cause of the problem, you may end up solving a symptom, but not resolving the underlying issue. If you spackle a cracked wall in your house, you can mask the problem, but it will crack again if you have a shifting foundation that needs to be repaired. Your employee is in the same situation. You can temporarily change some behavior, but if the root cause of the problem remains untouched, you'll experience problems with this employee over and over again. You won't always be able to completely fix the problem, but understanding the cause will help you be a more effective manager.

There are certain problems you can't solve for your employee, particularly ones that stem from personality traits or from personal problems the employee is dealing with. Karen noticed that Peggy was always late for a Monday morning meeting scheduled at 8 A.M. Peggy was a key component to the meeting and starting without her or waiting until she got there was a problem for the team, which was on a tight schedule. Karen talked to Peggy to find out what was going on. Peggy explained that she has to get her kids on the bus on Monday mornings, since her husband has to be at work early.

If you are aware of a situation such as Peggy's, you have the power to decide if you want to work around it. But if you have no idea why she's always late, you have no ability to change the situation. You, as a manager, would need to decide if Peggy is so valuable to you that you want to change the time of the meeting, or if the team's schedule is more important and Peggy has to find a way to get there or she will no longer be able to keep her position.

EFFECT ON YOUR TEAM AND COMPANY

You've heard the saying that a bad apple can spoil the whole bunch. When you have a subpar employee, there is the chance that he could have a negative impact on your team and your company. A bad apple is bad for everyone, whether he causes an emotional drain on the people on the team, a drain on resources, or negatively affects the company's bottom line.

It may not seem to be such a big deal that Jan spends a lot of time with personal e-mail, or that Rory makes negative comments in meetings. However, this behavior not only reduces the amount of actual work that employee is doing, but may also taint the attitude of the rest of your team. If team members see that Joy never fully completes the purchase orders and that no one cares, your other employees are going to wonder why they're working so hard to complete their own P.O.s and may start to slack off.

Then there is the employee who has a bad attitude about everything. If there is one person who always sees the glass as half empty, he's going to share his negative views with the rest of your team. Negativity is insidious. It can easily become part of your team or company culture. One employee who is always negative will eventually wear down the positive attitudes of those around him, and your entire team will end up behaving in a negative manner.

9

BAD TO THE CORE OR JUST BRUISED?

We all know that people make mistakes and that none of our employees are perfect. You can't expect perfection, but you can expect solid, dependable work. You can also look for progress after mistakes are made—an employee who learns from her mistakes is a valuable team member.

If you have an employee who slips up and makes an error or does something wrong, you'll probably be annoyed, but most of the time it's not a reason to spring into action and analyze whether the person should be fired. It's counterproductive to overreact to every problem that happens with your employees. If you are looking for problems, you will no doubt find them, but if you expect the best, you will often get it.

There are some employees, though, who may begin to slip up habitually. A bad apple isn't someone who makes the occasional mistake, but the employee who has a distinct ongoing pattern of a certain type of behavior or failure.

One important clue that can help you sift out minor problems from ongoing patterns is the severity of the incidents. One slightly snitty e-mail is an incident; however a very nasty, inflammatory e-mail can be indicative of a potentially real problem. Once you've got two inflammatory e-mails, you're well on your way to a pattern.

It can sometimes be hard to tell if a pattern is developing with an employee. In the heat of the moment when you're dealing with the crisis in front of you, it can be hard to really see the big picture. The best way to evaluate the situation is to keep good records. Document every important mistake or problem that happens for every employee. If you simply rely on your memory or impressions, you cannot ensure the situation will be judged fairly and accurately. You may find that over the course of weeks, months, or a year, you'll see a clear pattern emerging in one person's file. A written record is important not only so you can know that you're not losing your mind (yes, Sheila did wear a see-through top to work three different times, you aren't crazy), but also so you can provide documentation should you reach the point where you need to fire the offender. Try to document as much detail about each occurrence as possible.

Things to make note of include:

- Who was involved (other employees, clients, vendors)?
- What time of day or day of the week did it occur?
- What was the situation that led up to the incident?
- What was the negative result?
- What action did you take?

These records can also help you determine a course of action to correct a problem. For example, at a small law firm, when the receptionist is off for the day, one of the legal assistants will fill in at the front desk. The legal assistants who are there when the firm opens in the morning decide among themselves who will fill that role. Without documentation, you may not be able to confirm that Barb always happens to come in late on the days when everyone knows the receptionist is going to be out so she doesn't have to take a turn working from the front desk. This might not seem like a big deal at first, but when you take into consideration that she never volunteers for any other shared responsibilities within the company, it becomes a bigger concern.

THE DIFFERENCE BETWEEN ANNOYING AND BAD

We all have employees who get on our nerves or who have personalities that drive us right up a tree. You can't like everyone.

You can, however, find a way to work with almost anyone. An employee whom you dislike on a personal level can still be a valuable part of your team or company. It can be hard to make the distinction, though, between someone who just gets under your skin and someone who is a liability to your team or your company. Employees who annoy members of your team can be a problem, but you need to weigh the impact of the annoyance against the employee's value to the company.

Try to look at the situation objectively and ask yourself these questions:

- Is the person's behavior having an impact on productivity? When there is an impact on productivity, you have a problem that goes beyond a personal reaction. If the employee is not getting work done, or his behavior is causing other employees to not function well, it's a sign that you're dealing with a real problem that needs to be addressed.
- Is the employee's working environment creating the situation or is it the person? A person might be responding to pressures or situations in her work area or team. For example, an employee's work may improve if she is moved away from someone who is a distraction to her.
- Is the objectionable activity because of a personality trait and not a workplace skill problem? If the employee is getting her work done and fulfilling her requirements, the fact that she talks nonstop about her cats should not mean she is not a worthwhile employee.
- Can you change the behavior by the way you manage the person? If there is a way for you to adjust your management style and tactics to reduce the problem the person is creating, then the employee is salvageable.

apples to apples A CASE STUDY

Helene managed the accounting department at an ice skate manufacturing company. Dan, one of her team members, constantly made sarcastic remarks. It seemed that he made comments every few minutes throughout team meetings. Helene had a problem with sarcasm and his behavior really grated on her. She tried to brush it aside and not let it bother her, until she realized that his comments were having a negative impact on other members of the team. Some of the women on the team privately expressed to Helene that they no longer wanted to speak up in meetings because they were afraid of what Dan might say. Helene decided that Dan's remarks had crossed a line. It was one thing to be the sarcastic guy in the corner, but it was another to discourage other employees from participating in a meeting. Helene spoke to Dan about his remarks and stepped in every time he made a sarcastic comment. Soon his behavior stopped.

When you have an employee who annoys other members of your team, but not you, the problem may not seem as pressing—after all, she's not making *you* crazy. However, the impact on your team can be significant. When people argue at work, it is usually about small, seemingly insignificant things. But these small annoyances can lead to big blowups. For instance, one of the biggest problems in the workplace is people taking and eating other people's food. Studies have actually shown this to be the biggest complaint people have about their workplace. Now, this kind of problem does not have a direct impact on productivity, but it does increase tension on the team. If Omar is mad that Dara ate his turkey sandwich and Lee puts big notes on his food in the fridge that say "DO NOT EAT—THIS MEANS YOU," tensions in the office are going to be elevated. Because of this, productivity is going to be affected because everyone is spending so much time steaming about who ate his or her yogurt or taking up a lot of work time casually walking past the lunchroom to try to catch the thief.

Your role as a manager is to step in and establish boundaries that keep annoying behavior in check. What you're really doing is telling everyone to play nice with each other, but it can be helpful to take that a step further and make some hard-and-fast rules for people to follow.

Consider some of these rules that can help reduce tension:

- Everyone must put their initials on their food in the company fridge, and no one is to eat anyone else's food.
- No one can play music openly in his or her cubicle. If you want to listen to music, use headphones.
- Everyone must eat only in the lunchroom, so that work areas do not smell of food.
- Food garbage can only be thrown away in the lunchroom.
- Risqué photos or art cannot be displayed in cubicles.

Establishing boundaries such as these can keep annoying behavior to a minimum.

PERSONAL OPINIONS AND PROFESSIONAL JUDGMENT

It can be hard to separate your personal feelings from the choices you make as a manager. Who you are as a person shapes your management choices in many ways. It can influence who you hire and how you react to different situations. However, when you're dealing with employees who may be difficult, you need to find a way to separate your professional self from your personal self. Again, it's possible for you to dislike an employee as a person, yet still see her value to the company.

Productivity is the ultimate baseline in all of these decisions.

Being aware that you have some biases can help you minimize them even though it can be difficult for you to clearly see what they are. As a manager, you need to become self-aware. Question yourself and determine why you respond the way that you do. You might discover some hidden biases that are influencing your decisions.

apples to apples A CASE STUDY

Kelli managed a team of public relations specialists for a health insurance company. Many of her employees were young women. One employee, Isabelle, seemed to live a particularly wild lifestyle. She was always talking about how she went to clubs and got totally smashed. Kelli was horrified by the stories and wondered about whether she really wanted Isabelle on her team. Kelli talked to another manager in the company about her feelings. He asked her about Isabelle's job performance and, when Kelli thought about it, it was excellent. She was very professional and had placed many positive media mentions of their company. She never came to work hung over or drunk and her personal appearance was impeccable. In fact, when Kelli thought about it, Isabelle really did nothing at work that had a negative impact on the company. She realized that Isabelle's stories offended her on a personal level, but Isabelle was actually a very good employee.

RESPONSIBILITY FOR YOUR HIRES

If you are the one who hired the troublesome employee, you might feel guilty or responsible for his failure to perform. You might also be worried about how this will reflect on you in the eyes of your superiors and whether it will damage the confidence your other employees have in you. If you made a bad call on this, maybe your judgment isn't so good?

The thing to remember is that how you feel about the situation has to come second to what the best thing is for the company. You may have the impulse to try to help this person along, cover up her mistakes, or compensate for her inability to perform. This can actually backfire because your superiors will see that not only did you hire a bad employee, you tried to cover it up.

While it may seem admirable to cultivate and bring along a new employee whom you see as having potential, this may not always be the best thing for the company. The time and energy you use to get that person to the point where he is fulfilling his role might be better spent elsewhere. If you've hired an employee who has turned out to be a big mistake, it is far better to fire the employee and admit your error, than it is to allow your team to be compromised.

WHY FIRING MAY NOT BE AN OPTION

It sounds pretty simple. If someone is not a productive member of your team, get rid of him. Unfortunately things are rarely that easy. There are many reasons you may not be able to fire a team member, but they all boil down to two categories:

- The employee has some kind of value to the company.
- The employee has a personal relationship that makes firing impossible.

An employee who has value to the company may have to be retained because she generates revenue directly, is essential in the delivery of services to a client, has specialized knowledge of some system or program in your company, or works for much less than any replacement would. It is also possible that you cannot afford the time and expense involved in finding someone else to fill the position (or perhaps there is a shortage of people with the appropriate skill set and there simply aren't any available candidates). The only way to fire someone in one of these positions is to be able to show that it makes more economic sense to let the person go than to keep him. You should take into account the soft economic impact as well, such as the influence on other employees' productivity and the potential costs of opportunities lost or missed.

An employee who has a personal relationship that prevents firing could be a friend or relative of your boss or other important person in your company, have a special relationship with a client that means he would take that business with him, or have some kind of ammunition against you or your boss that makes firing impossible. The economic argument is your strongest one if you are trying to find a way to get this person fired, but you have to be aware that you can damage your own position in the company if you suggest to your boss that his cousin should be let go. The more connected the person is and the higher up on the corporate ladder that connection is, the stronger your economic argument must be.

apples to apples A CASE STUDY

Amber has a close relationship with a key buyer for her company's largest customer and it is clear that the buyer would follow her if she left. Her manager, Sarah, feels as if she can't get rid of Amber even though she doesn't give the same level of service to other customers and orders from those customers are dwindling. Since Sarah can't fire Amber right now, she brainstorms ways to change things so Amber doesn't have so much power. She looks for ways to introduce other buyers and decision-makers to that key customer. By reworking the situation, Sarah changed the dynamic so that many people in her company talk to many who work for the largest customer. That way, she no longer feels as if Amber is holding a gun to her head.

Bad apples exist and, at some point in your career, you're going to have to find a way to deal with them. In *some* situations you may have to accept that you can't fire the employee. You must move on and find a way to make this person work for, rather than against, you. But before you take action, it's helpful to know that there are many different types of bad apples out there and many different ways to deal with them.

CHAPTER 2

TYPES OF BAD APPLES

There are a lot of different categories of bad apples—after all, every employee is an individual and can become a problem in his or her own special way. No matter what type of difficult employee you encounter as a manager, there are some basic strategies that you can employ.

CH 1. What Is a Bad Apple?

CH 2. Types of Bad Apples

CH 3. Bad Apples You Inherit

CH 4. Bad Apples Outside of Your Control

IDENTIFY THE ISSUES

First, get your facts together. Isolate exactly what the person has done, said, failed to do, or influenced and be able to identify when it happened and how it happened. Next, identify how the behavior, failure, or activity has had a negative impact on the company or team. Determine what the right strategy is for dealing with the situation. You can't create a written report every time one employee annoys another or creates a small problem. Instead, weigh the severity of the incidents and take action in concordance with the importance.

Once you have your strategy straight in your mind, talk with your employee. Explain exactly what your concern is and point out how it has harmed the company or team. Then, offer some suggestions as to how the employee can change his behavior to avoid these problems in the future. Again, make sure you document every important incident and every conversation so you'll have a record if you reach the point where you need to fire someone. Your HR department may have specific guidelines to follow, so be sure to follow company procedures.

GOSSIPS

There are gossips in every workplace and it's true that almost everyone enjoys a bit of gossip now and then. There are two kinds of gossips. The first is the blabbermouth who wants to talk about everything—people in the office, celebrities, her neighbors, her kids' friends, and so on. This kind of a gossip can be a problem if all of her constant talking becomes a distraction for herself or for other team members.

The best strategy for a blabbermouth is to remind her to get back on track. If it becomes such a problem that you need to have a discussion with her, tell her that it's fine for her to chat about anything during her breaks, but you expect her to concentrate on work during the workday.

The other type of gossip is the workplace gossip. This kind of employee talks about people in the office, spreads rumors, picks apart people's personal lives, and focuses on who said what, wore what, did what, or acted how at work. This is not only a waste of work time, but can also make other people in the workplace very uncomfortable. Not only do you need to remind this person to focus on work, but you may also need to remind her that, from an HR standpoint, it's inappropriate to discuss other people's personal lives at the office.

apples to apples A CASE STUDY

Cheryl works at an ad agency and loves gossip. Cheryl overheard Carrie on the phone and thought she heard her say that she was pregnant. Cheryl couldn't wait to share this juicy tidbit and made a beeline for the ladies' room, where she promptly told her pal from HR, as well as several other women. Soon, it was all over the company that Carrie was pregnant. Her boss heard and started to think about how he would fill her job while she was out. Several people even talked about how they would like Carrie's job. Eventually, at lunch one day, Carrie mentioned her sister was pregnant. Someone piped up and said how nice that she and her sister would have babies so close together. Carrie had no idea what the woman was talking about and made it clear she wasn't pregnant. Gossips like Cheryl can be dangerous. Not only can they spread rumors that aren't true, but can sometimes cause serious damage to a coworker's reputation.

Some people just need to talk and, if you can help channel the gossip toward other topics, you may find it fills that need. Make it clear that your gossiper can talk all she wants about her own personal life or things she is doing, but that the personal lives of other people in the office are off-limits. You can also rearrange the workplace so that the opportunity for constant conversation is reduced—for example, moving a blabbermouth away from the copy machine to a more remote area of the team space may help reduce her opportunity for constant chattering. How you explain to her why you are moving her depends on whether putting it all on the table will help or not. Telling her you're doing this may then mean she will get up often in order to go chat or take a break, whereas before she at least stayed at her desk.

BACKSTABBER

The backstabber is a person who throws other people under the bus to get ahead, but in a sneaky, behind-the-scenes manner. He'll support an idea at a meeting, but will come to you later to say that he's given it some thought and doesn't think David has the skills to handle the project. A backstabber undermines team spirit and makes it impossible for your team to trust and support each other. One backstabber often creates a culture of backstabbing, since everyone feels they have to protect themselves at all times.

Don't Get Backstabbed
Keep in mind that someone who is backstabbing other team members is just as likely to be undermining you. Keep a close eye on this employee and how she portrays you to others. This is not someone you should trust easily.

The best way to deal with a backstabber is to first stop enabling the behavior. Don't let Marisa come into your office and privately tell you her concerns about Rick's design for a client's website. Instead, tell her that if she needs to comment about it, she can do so at the team meeting.

If the backstabbing continues, sit the person down and point out what he is doing. Think about his motivation—is he trying to get ahead, discredit an enemy, or does he simply not have the interpersonal skills to deal with conflict face to face? Once you've determined the reason for the behavior, you can offer the person a different path to achieve that goal. If he's trying to get ahead, show him other routes to success. If he's dealing with conflict with another employee, have HR try to smooth things out. If he's afraid of conflict, help him learn how to voice his concerns in a nonconfrontational way and be there to control the conversation when it happens.

PASSIVE-AGGRESSIVE

The passive-aggressive employee is one who is stubborn, sullen, and silently resentful. She is the employee who agrees to take on a certain task and then "forgets" because she didn't really want to do it in the first place, but didn't want to say no. These employees express aggression in covert, silent ways or through sins of omission. Instead of letting you know that a project isn't within their area of expertise or comfort zone, they may do things poorly in the hope that they won't have to do it again. This type of behavior can really have an impact on productivity because the employee's lack of action may not be evident immediately and can create gaps that have significant effects on other people in the team.

To deal with this type of behavior, determine why the employee is forgetting, and not participating or completing tasks fully.

There isn't always a good explanation—often people who behave in a passive-aggressive way don't understand the reasons behind their behavior.

apples to apples A CASE STUDY

Elaine, who has never liked Marcia, answers the phone while Marcia is at lunch and "forgets" to write a phone message about a change to a purchase order that Marcia is responsible for. Marcia never gets the information and the order doesn't get shipped to the right place. Marcia looks bad to their boss, but Elaine says it was a simple mistake. One incident like this is not a problem, but a pattern of these passive mistakes fueled by malintent is indicative of something that needs to be addressed.

Your first step as a manager is to make the passive-aggressive person aware that you see a pattern and won't accept her excuses. You need to go over the standard office procedures with her again—how phone messages must be recorded, where orders are to be filed, and so on, so that she can't claim ignorance or forgetfulness. Make sure that there are written procedures available for her (and the rest of your team) to reference. This can eliminate the "I haven't done this in so long that I simply forgot" excuse. If there is a pattern of incidents, you need to create a record of them. If you can't fire Elaine in the example, maybe you need to make some changes so that Elaine doesn't have the potential to screw up Marcia's work. You could have someone else answer the phone, route Marcia's orders through someone else on the team, etc.

When dealing with a passive-aggressive employee, make it clear that you recognize the behavior for what it is—a refined attempt to cause damage without being obvious. Make sure the person understands that you're watching and are aware of what's going on. Once she knows you have your eye on her, it takes away her cover and exposes her bad apple behavior.

WASTER

There are two types of wasters. A time waster is someone who does not use time at work well. He's the employee who spends way too much time at the coffee machine, delivering documents to another department, checking his e-mail, or cleaning out his desk. A time waster needs you to set specific goals for him and then follow up on them. He needs to understand how much he should be doing and be held accountable for that work. He often needs to be redirected to get back to work. You may walk by the water cooler and notice him there yet again. Sometimes a look is all that is needed; other times you may need to tell him it's time to get back to work. This kind of attention will either result in a change in behavior or make the employee decide to leave because there is too much pressure.

Don't confuse the time waster with someone who is having trouble with his work, though. If an employee is feeling overwhelmed or unprepared to deal with a problem or project, his reaction may be to avoid it and diddle around with other things. Always be sure your employee has the skills and resources needed to complete the work. Check in with your team members on a regular basis to find out how things are going and how they are feeling about their jobs. Encourage them to come to you with problems or concerns. If they aren't able to do something, you want them to know they can talk about it instead of sitting at their desk, sharpening pencils to look busy.

The other kind of waster is a resource waster. Linda likes to print the agenda for the internal meetings in color, which costs four times as much as black and white. Wasters may use up too many supplies, but they may also waste other people's time—another important company resource. If Anthony always asks another team employee to make sure the scanner is set up correctly before he scans in documents (especially if he always does it right, but just wants someone to double-check), this is a drain on company resources that can ultimately affect productivity.

Resource wasters may not even be aware of what they are doing, so a quick word with the employee may solve the problem. Another solution is to put forward a big push for your entire team to be "green" and use fewer resources. If the entire team is helping one another be more green, the peer pressure will be a great motivator. If this isn't helpful, you may have to make people sign out supplies. You can even monitor the amount of printing each employee is doing by setting up user profiles for the printer. Once employees know that they'll be monitored, they often shape up pretty quickly.

NARCISSIST

The narcissist is someone who thinks only of himself or who sees himself as the ultimate savior for the team—the lynchpin in the entire process. A narcissist needs to be educated about the importance of each member of the team and the interdependence of everyone at the company. You can do this by stressing teamwork and cooperation.

apples to apples A CASE STUDY

Connor is a project engineer who always makes sure that he's the one to hand the completed project scope to the sales department for presentation to the client. He sees his contributions as the most important and fails to think about the project as a whole or consider other people's contributions. Because of this, he doesn't always highlight the most important points, and fails to give the sales department the best talking points for presentation. And because he isn't thorough enough, the sales department ends up giving incomplete information to the clients about the projects, and sales are lost.

Think about the person's motivation. If Connor engages in bad apple behavior to get accolades from the sales team for his work, then you, as his manager, need to create a process that allows the entire team to work up a talking point presentation, so that credit won't be given to just one person. If this isn't possible, or you don't want to work around Connor's issues, tell him you want to see talking points that list contributions from all team members, with an annotation as to who is responsible for what. You could also change the process so that each team member has a turn submitting to the sales team.

When working with a narcissist, remember that he is approaching things with a bias. He may not intentionally be trying to make himself look good, but he may simply have a mindset in which he only thinks about his role, his impact, and his situation. He may not intend to give short shrift to others, but the result of his limited vision is that others are harmed.

Some narcissists behave this way because their ultimate goal is to make their own jobs easier because nothing else is important. They don't care about getting praise or looking good, but they want to get things arranged so that their own job is less work, less stressful, or easier, and the impact on other people doesn't matter. Getting your narcissist to be more aware of other people is a difficult challenge because this is an ingrained personality type. Your only option may be to work around it.

THE LIAR

The workplace liar is the guy who won't admit he used up the toner in the copier and didn't replace it, claims he never received the team e-mail about the change in deadlines, and makes promises he has no intention of keeping. Liars are also known for telling inflated stories about themselves, and they end up having a reputation as being full of you-know-what. Other times, this is the guy who lies to cover his butt at every opportunity. No matter what kinds of lies he tells, he'll never actually admit that he lied, so trying to get an admission is not going to be helpful.

You have two choices with a liar. You can confront him, call him on his lie, and let him know that you won't accept any more untruths. This approach should be used for significant lies, which have an important impact on the company or other employees. You can also advise him that if his behavior doesn't change, you may have to change his role to avoid situations in which a lie could have a big impact.

Sometimes, however, it doesn't pay to get into a big confrontation. Your team may be annoyed that he lied about ordering more paper towels for the kitchen, but it probably doesn't have a direct impact on your company's success. If you've got a minor liar, you may just choose to turn a blind eye to the problem and realize that you must take whatever he tells you with a grain of salt. You will quickly start discounting what he says and stop going to him for important information. The team will also quickly see this happening. They will stop valuing what he says. This peer pressure may be just what is needed to get him to stop.

LAZY BONES

The lazy employee is one who is always looking for the easy way to do something. If your team has a ten-step procedure for getting job site approval for a building, your lazy employee may decide to cut out steps four and five because they're too much work. The lazy employee doesn't feel a sense of urgency about any task and gets to it when she gets to it. She never does anything extra and sets the bar for performance at the minimal level of acceptable.

apples to apples A CASE STUDY

Kara has a habit of sending interoffice e-mails about customer problems without giving the exact name of the company or the customer number. Instead of titling her e-mail "Re: Northeastern Auction Services," she might call them NE Services, Northeastern, N. Auctions, Auctions, or some other abbreviation. She doesn't take the time to get the correct name of the client and assumes that everyone knows what she's talking about. Most of the time they do, but if they also had a customer called Northeast Trucking Services, this could result in big mixups that would have been avoided if she weren't so lazy. To get her to work harder, her manager Aaron discovered what motivates Kara and used it as a carrot on a stick to get the performance he needed.

This bad apple is lazy because she doesn't have the proper motivation. If promotions or merit increases are something that employee is interested in, point out that laziness that causes problems for the company will have a negative impact on those goals when it comes time for performance reviews. Some people aren't interested in promotions, so you need to make simply keeping their job an important goal. Sometimes, a very clear standard operating procedure can give a lazy person clear and unmistakable hoops to jump through. Part of the problem with lazy employees is that they are often too lazy to take the time to think something through. If you do the thinking for them, and clearly lay out exactly what they need to do, they will often respond.

COMBATANTS

Some employees are aggressive and always looking to challenge people, or start arguments, which can be damaging to your team morale. Your other employees will start anticipating the arguments and find ways to back away from them before they start. By turning everything into a challenge, a combatant on your team can make things exhausting for everyone.

apples to apples A CASE STUDY

Bryan is an advertising spot writer for a radio station. During brainstorming meetings, a lot of ideas are thrown out by everyone on the team. Even if everyone else can agree, Bryan continues to fight for his idea, which makes meetings last forever. Instead of spending time refining the chosen idea, the team ends up arguing over which idea they're going to go with. As the team manager, you need to limit the amount of debate time available. Make it clear there will only be ten minutes of discussion before a decision is reached. Encourage Bryan to channel his passion into supporting and shaping the idea the team is going to work on, even if it isn't his.

When you have an aggressive team member, you need to be the one who steps in and stops the fighting before it begins. End the meeting, change the subject, or point out that there is no need to get angry or upset. If this kind of behavior continues, talk privately with the aggressor and let him know that it's fine to raise questions and offer his opinion, but that he cannot intimidate other employees, become angry, or raise his voice. Laying some strict boundaries will help him understand what kind of behavior is acceptable at work.

POISONER

Closely related to the combatant, this person sees her role as the devil's advocate. No idea is ever good enough and no solution is right; the glass is half-empty. She enjoys the turmoil and stress of a chaotic situation and tries to undermine progress at every step. She finds a problem with everything, rarely contributes in a positive way, and you can count on her to point out the negatives of every decision. We all complain about the weather sometimes, but when it's a nice day we enjoy it. She's the one who says, "Yes, it's a nice day, but I hear it's going to rain tomorrow." She finds something to be unhappy or negative about in every situation.

The problem with a poisoner is not only her bad attitude, but, by constantly finding problems and negatives, she can turn the entire mindset of your team around so everyone is negative. One poisoner can turn a roomful of positive people into naysayers.

apples to apples A CASE STUDY

A decision was made by a sports memorabilia auction house to start taking American Express in addition to Visa and MasterCard. Chandra hears about it and immediately begins telling others in the accounting department that it's a bad idea because it will make it harder for all of them to balance the books at the end of every day. She talks about how few people really use American Express anyhow, and having to change their procedure to accommodate it is a waste of their time. Soon, other people agree with her and the whole department is up in arms about this small change. If Chandra hadn't poisoned the situation, everyone would have done the small extra step without comment.

You don't want to stifle anyone's viewpoint—having different viewpoints can be beneficial. However, this bad apple is not in any way constructive. As a manager, you need to express your appreciation for looking at things from different angles, but stress that employees need to contribute solutions rather than problems. It's fine for employees to express concerns, but there must also be a willingness to find a way to make the decision work.

Getting employees invested in the decision-making process can also prevent poisoning from happening. People are less likely to criticize something they had some say in.

You may need to point out to the poisoner that her first instinct is to criticize and raise all the negative points about decisions. She can be encouraged to try to think more positively some of the time and perhaps will learn to keep some of her criticisms to herself.

THE BULLY

A bully is the employee who always must get his way. He excessively criticizes others and pushes at them until they cave in to what he wants. He stops at nothing and may steal things, curse, shout, use the silent treatment, do things to hurt people's feelings, or even physically shove someone to get his way.

Rampant Bullying

A study at Arizona State University revealed that between 25 and 30 percent of all employees have been bothered by a bully at work at some point in their working career.

Bullying cannot be tolerated in the workplace. You, as a manager, must document the incidents (which can be hard since many people who are bullied never come forward) and then find a way to fire the bully. Try to watch for the aftereffects of a bullying incident. If you find at meetings that all eyes look to a specific person for his thoughts before anyone else speaks, this can mean the person is a leader among the group *or* it may be that this person is a bully whom no one wants to get in the way of. If you notice that no one offers any constructive criticism of or differing views from a specific team member, this also can be a sign of previous bullying.

If you suspect bullying, you need to closely monitor team communication. Read their e-mail, stand nearby and listen to their conversations, and observe what is happening. If you can't fire this bad apple once he's identified, separate him from the team so he cannot wield his influence as strongly. You can also talk with him and point out what he's doing. Tell him you expect more cooperation from him. Threats of reduction in job responsibility and other consequences may help him see the error of his ways.

THE SLOB

The slob can take on several manifestations. First, there is the person who cannot keep his work area neat, and may also make messes in common areas. His cubicle is filled with empty soda cans, piles of paper, broken pencils, baseball caps, and unidentifiable objects. The work area slob may offend others around him who think his area is making the whole place look like a pigsty, and they may be angry about his inability to clean up after himself in common areas. His sloppiness may have an impact on his job performance because he loses things, misplaces documents, and can't get organized.

Getting this employee back on track may simply require you telling him he has one day to clean up his area. It may also require telling the entire team that each person is required to clean up after himself in the common areas.

Another kind of slob is the personal appearance or hygiene slob. Chloe may be a fantastic worker, but if she wears dirty clothes, has bad breath, or gross dandruff, she can be a complete turnoff to clients. If you have this kind of situation, try to get HR involved because you don't want to risk saying the wrong thing. This kind of slob has to be encouraged to take more time with her appearance or hygiene. If you're in a small company and have no HR department, you can give the entire team a pep talk about what a professional appearance is and how to maintain one.

A slob may also be someone who scribbles notes illegibly or incompletely when having to convey information. In this case, you need to explain that her writing is making it difficult for other people to act on the information and that she needs to either take more effort in writing or use electronic means (e-mail, Word documents, etc.). She may misfile things or misplace documents or files. This type of slob needs reminders to put things back where they go and can benefit from a clearly laid-out organizational plan.

THIEF

Thieves are known for stealing material possessions. If your coffee cup is missing, there's a good chance he took it. If you can't find the stapler, it's most likely on her desk or in her drawer. If you're dealing with this type of bad apple, make sure that possessions are clearly labeled and if that means everyone needs to put their initials on their rulers, then that's what has to happen. If the issue is one of convenience, make sure everyone has his or her own stuff. If that means buying an extra stapler for your bad apple, do so. But many times, this same person will simply lose track of things and have to "borrow" from someone else. If this problem persists, inventory what you've provided for each person and require them to pay for replacement of the items. Obviously, if personal or company items are stolen, you cannot tolerate this and immediate action must be taken.

There's another category of thief as well—the idea thief. She not only steals other people's brilliant ideas and presents them as her own, but she's also not above taking credit for work other people did. This can cause significant resentment from other team members, as well as lead you to mistakenly elevate the thief to responsibilities she is not really able to handle. If you suspect this is happening, ask some deeper questions about an idea she is presenting. Try to find out how she came up with the idea. If it always seems that the idea just came to her, this may be a sign that others did the heavy lifting and she just picked it up at the end. You can also challenge her on the idea, making her defend it. If she is not able to articulate why it is a good idea or is quick to move off it, it may show that she didn't really come up with it. If this is the case, require her to offer more details on ideas submitted in the future. This can force her to be more invested earlier in the idea development. Also, explain that misrepresentations of this type hurt both her and the company.

WHINER

You can hear the whiner in your head. Why do we have to do it this waaaaayyy? Jenny left early for the day, why can't IIIII? Your first inclination might be to tell her to grow up, but this generally doesn't work. You can, however, cut her off at the pass. Proactively explain to the entire team a decision, new policy, etc., and the process that resulted in the outcome. If appropriate, indicate who was involved and, at the first sign of a whine, interject that you don't expect to hear any whining about the situation. Let her (and the whole team) know you will be happy to listen to constructive input, but otherwise, it is best to focus on moving forward.

It's also important to understand why people whine. Maybe they feel unimportant or uninvolved. Try to get these people involved early so they'll feel that they own some of the responsibility and will then have less incentive to whine.

Some people, no matter how you explain things or direct them, will always find something to whine about. You may at some point have to have a talk with a person like this to point out the behavior; say that it's distracting the entire team and has to stop.

UNRELIABLE/INCOMPETENT

This kind of employee is the one who either can't be trusted to get anything done or is simply unable to get anything done. You need to strongly consider this person's value to the company. If you must keep him, determine if it is a skill set (or lack thereof) or a personality issue that's causing the problem. If it's a personality issue, bring it to the person's attention and develop a strategy to help him improve. If it is a skill-set issue, training or mentoring may be the right answer. Many times, when given access to additional knowledge and the experience of a successful employee, this bad apple can see real approaches that he never considered. Be sure you select the right mentor. A mentor must be a willing participant, otherwise you risk creating another bad apple. If you don't see results, you will have to look for areas where the incompetent employee's impact and responsibility is minimized.

CAREER CLIMBER

You've seen this kind of employee. She's interested only in furthering her own career. She's not going to be stuck in this stupid job in this Podunk company for long. She's always thinking about how to look better, get recognition, and shoot up the company organizational chart. And it doesn't matter at whose expense that promotion will be.

This person has some positives—she is motivated to do a good job to get ahead, is an avid learner, and will not shy away from a challenge or opportunity to shine on a tough project. The downside is that she generally only looks out for herself and has little regard for whom or what she steps on in her way to the top.

The first step is to recognize this type of employee for what she is. Then you can manage her activity and responsibilities to the benefit of the team and company. Be sure she isn't distracted by taking on more work than she can effectively handle, or by projects and tasks outside her core responsibilities. Monitor her activity with outside vendors, companies, and clients. She will always be fishing for a better job and many times that is her primary focus in interactions with clients and vendors. Long lunches, meetings, or phone calls with the same client, where no real need is established or no outcome can be gained, may be signs that something is going on.

To protect yourself, make sure that this bad apple doesn't have exclusive knowledge about key business operations and procedures. She should also not be the only contact an important customer has with your company.

If you believe this employee is a long-term asset to the company, try to develop a longer-term career path within your company for her. Be open about your willingness to help her advance. If there isn't a way to keep her long term, discuss this with her also. Recognize that she will eventually outgrow her position or the company itself, and work with her to plan for this inevitable transition. This can mean she will give you a longer window to find a replacement than the standard two weeks, which can definitely make your life easier.

OUR LADY OF PERPETUAL CRISIS

Don't let the title of this one fool you—this bad apple can be a man or a woman. Some employees live their lives in a state of constant crisis. For some, their personal life is in turmoil, or else they lead you to believe it is. This is the employee who takes six days off in one month because his wife is sick, his dog ran away, his car broke down, he sprained his ankle, and his house has termites.

If you think you've got someone who fits this mold, talk to him. Provide an outline of each incident so that the pattern becomes obvious. It's likely he's not even aware of it because he is so caught up in the crisis of the day, hour, or minute. Explain what kind of impact his actions are having on the team and the company. You probably need to review with him company policies related to time off, flexible scheduling, and so on, so he understands what the rules are. It is also important to let him know that, while you understand and appreciate the issues confronting him in his personal life, you have an obligation to keep everyone focused on the company's issues when at work. You can also let him know that you're sorry he's facing such difficult problems, but at some point he's got to make a decision as to whether he can really fulfill the job requirements.

The other crisis employee is the one who makes everything at work into a crisis. Oh my gosh! The copier is out of paper and the agenda for the client meeting needs to be printed *right* now! The website is down, the help desk phone goes right to voicemail, and there's no one to help me! This kind of employee blows every little thing into a giant disaster. She's always upset and worried—and expects you to be, too. She wants everyone else to fix her crisis of the moment.

You need to help this person understand how to put things into perspective. Remind her to take a deep breath to interrupt the escalating panic; then, teach her to focus on identifying concrete steps she can take to resolve each problem. For example, if the website's down, she should leave a clear, concise voicemail. She should take note of when she called and call them back if they don't return her call. Find out if there are other contacts at the company that she can reach out to outside the help desk. In many cases, it is a matter of helping the employee mentally map out the steps that she needs to take to deal with a problem, as well as creating a series of alternatives if each step does not resolve the problem.

THE JOB HATER

This job sucks! You may have a bad apple who is known to say that and other negative things about the company, job, or work at hand. This person is determined to be eternally miserable, no matter what happens. He just hates to work. It's tempting to let him be miserable or wait for him to finally quit, but in the meantime he can significantly bring down the team's morale.

Take this employee aside and say you've heard him complain about his job. Ask him what exactly is wrong. What does he hate about it? Why? How could things be made better? Most likely, everything will be outside his control. Urge him to identify things within his control that can make things better; then help him implement these solutions. You may be able to have some impact on the things that are outside of his control, but you'll need to weigh how valuable he is to your team against the effort it would take to make the changes he wants. If you can't or won't make changes, he will need to learn to cope with the fact that some things in life are not perfect. Help him learn to emphasize the positives whenever you can.

Remember, no matter what type of difficult employee you encounter as a manager, there are basic strategies that you can employ to get them back in line. But what happens when you have to recognize and manage a bad apple you've inherited?

CHAPTER 3

BAD APPLES YOU INHERIT

When you are promoted within your company or are hired from outside to fill a management position, you usually inherit a team that is already in place. In many ways this can be a blessing. You have a group of people who already know how to do their jobs, understand what is expected, and can be helpful in showing you the ropes if necessary. Sometimes, however, one of the employees on your team is one you would never have hired had you been given the option. Learning how to manage employees like these is an important skill.

CH 1. What Is a Bad Apple?

CH 2. Types of Bad Apples

CH 3. Bad Apples You Inherit

CH 4. Bad Apples Outside of Your Control

ASSESS STRENGTHS AND WEAKNESSES

When you move into a new position, one of the first things you should do is evaluate the strengths and weaknesses of all of your new employees. You need to get to know the company, the jobs, and the requirements that your team is dealing with. You can't effectively evaluate anyone until you understand what his or her jobs entail. This is true even if you are promoted from within the company. Try to take a fresh look at things and don't make assumptions just because you're familiar with the surroundings or people. To be a good manager you need a discerning eye.

Promotion from Within

If you were promoted from within the company you may think you already have a handle on what members of the team are good employees and which ones aren't. But, in actuality, you really do need to completely reassess the situation once you're in your new job. The way you interacted with people— and the way you saw their performance—was much different when you were working side by side.

It can also be challenging to be suddenly managing someone who was your friend when you were both part of a team. You may not have minded that Lucy was completely lazy about work because it really didn't affect you. However, now that you're responsible for her output, you've got to be able to talk with her about your concerns and work through the problems.

DO YOUR HOMEWORK

Start with the files. Read each job description carefully and check out the personnel files for each employee. Then meet with each person individually—if you are able to take each person outside of the office for a cup of coffee, you're more likely to have an informative meeting. Have a friendly conversation about his role on the team. Ask what she likes and doesn't like about the job and areas she sees for improvement. Find out what she sees as her role within the team and company; compare it to the job description you have. Many times, the original job description is no longer accurate, so you need to either update the description or change the person's responsibilities. These conversations will be revealing, but you want to be careful to not immediately pigeonhole anyone as a bad employee. Instead, gather information that will eventually lead you to an informed opinion.

Be aware that a potentially bad employee may try to cover up his bad habits, so try to be sure the information you are getting is accurate. A red flag will go up if the person is telling you one thing but you're seeing something different.

apples to apples A CASE STUDY

Kiran was hired as managing editor at a magazine and took the time to meet with all of the editors underneath her. She made a point to ask them about their job responsibilities and how well they felt they were fulfilling them. Jesse presented a glowing picture of his work at the magazine. He said he didn't feel there were any problems. He claimed that everything in his department ran smoothly. This was in direct contrast to what Kiran had observed. Jesse was always late turning in the copy for his department. His assistants were always rushing and the copy was riddled with mistakes. Kiran made note of the discrepancy between what he told her and what she saw and decided to keep a close eye on him and his work since she felt it was likely he might be a potential problem for her. In this instance, recognizing a potential bad apple allowed Kiran to take Jesse aside and set deadlines and goals to get his work back on track.

SET GOALS

Once you have a sense as to how each person fits into the team, you should set goals for each employee. Goals are important because they provide a specific target that an employee can focus on to keep on track. They also offer a tangible yardstick that you can use to evaluate performance in the future. This can help you as you determine if someone is a bad apple and define what activity or attitude makes them one.

It's important to involve the employees when setting goals. You want their input and ideas about what they can accomplish and how they can get there. There are some bad apple signs to watch out for at this stage. Employees who do the following may be problems:

- Balk at and seem unwilling to set goals
- Have no idea how to set goals
- Set goals that are obviously too low
- Establish goals that are impossible to meet

Observe your new employees as they work toward their goals. Failure to achieve them will serve as a warning sign for you. As your employees work, take note of their strengths and weaknesses. You may even ask them to evaluate themselves and identify areas where they need improvement. All employees have weaknesses—a weakness is not a sign that someone is a bad employee. However, an employee who is not willing to work to improve upon a weakness can be a potential problem.

The types of goals you should set include team goals and individual goals. Your first order of business is to encourage your employees to maintain current levels of productivity. You don't want to walk in the door as a new manager and tell everyone that what they are doing is not good enough. Eventually, you'll want your team to increase productivity, but for now, if what they are doing works, ask them to continue.

It is not uncommon to find that your team has become complacent under the former manager. In this situation, you will need to re-energize them and make sure everyone is interested in achieving team success. Remember though, it will take time for them to adjust to your new expectations and requirements.

When you have identified a troublesome employee, you will want to work with her to set goals as well. Goals for bad employees can be as straightforward as telling a liar to be as accurate as possible in what she says. Another employee may need more complicated goals, such as a detailed plan for how he can start to show improvement and increased ability. You can also take a bad employee and use him as inspiration for helping the entire team improve. For example, if you have a slob on your team, you can use it as an opportunity to define for the entire team what business casual is—what kind of attire is appropriate—without singling out your slob directly.

MANAGE WITH STRENGTHS AND WEAKNESSES IN MIND

Part of your job as a manager is to put your employees into situations where they can best use their skills and abilities. If you see that Tim struggles with public speaking, don't require him to give the presentation to the client if you have someone else who is available, more comfortable, and can do a better job. Forcing Tim to give the presentation is not the best use of him as a resource. Your goal should be to match skills to tasks, so that the people who are the most skilled at certain tasks are the people who are usually assigned to those tasks.

But keep in mind there's a fine line here between optimizing your employees' skills and letting their weaknesses control your management decisions. If no one else is available to give the presentation and it is part of Tim's job responsibilities, you should require him to do it (this will be part of flushing out bad employees—holding them to the job descriptions when necessary and letting them sink or swim). However, when you can rely on your employees' strengths it will mean that the work the team produces will be better and usually be completed more efficiently. Good employees who are constantly asked to do things they don't like or aren't good at will soon become dissatisfied employees.

You should also manage with an eye toward helping your employees improve on their weaknesses. This doesn't mean simply telling someone to shape up. Instead, offer help and resources that allow them to improve their skills. By doing so, you can help prevent the downward slide that sometimes happens when an employee feels overwhelmed or underskilled.

This approach can also help change a bad inherited employee into a good employee. If the previous manager created an environment of stress and dissatisfaction by requiring work outside of what the employee was capable of, this probably resulted in negative responses, which likely became habits. By placing people in positions where they can succeed, their attitude will improve with each success and you may be able to eliminate the bad apple responses.

CREATING RELATIONSHIPS WITH INHERITED EMPLOYEES

You can minimize the potential for difficult behavior with your new employees by starting things off on the right foot. Making your expectations clear from the beginning will ensure that everyone is on the same page.

UNDERSTAND DYNAMICS

There are several situations that might have an impact on the way your team is reacting to you and your hiring. Understanding these dynamics can help you understand the behavior you are seeing, or even anticipate it.

apples to apples A CASE STUDY

Before Rachel was hired, Chad applied for her position. Chad had a hard time with the fact that he was overlooked for this promotion and, as a result, started showing bad apple behavior. Once Rachel took the time to find out that he was considered and ultimately rejected for her position, she was better able to understand his behavior. She allowed Chad to get used to the idea that she was managing him instead of trying to force him to accept her immediately. This kind of respect ultimately garnered Chad's respect in return.

You may not know how to cope with this type of situation, but ignoring it won't help. Instead, develop a strategy to deal with these employees. Avoid saying anything that may appear insincere or gloating such as, "You know it could have gone either way" or

"You win some, you lose some." The key is to make sure you offer genuine respect to the person.

If your team had a very difficult boss before you, they may be conditioned to react in certain ways that send warning signals to you. If they assume that you will treat them the same way the previous boss did, they may be resentful, unmotivated, and display a lot of the bad apple behavior you're on the lookout for. You'll never know the reason for what you're seeing unless you take the time to get to know them and find out what working on the team was like under the old manager. Once you do that, take the opportunity to show them how things will be run from now on, preventing more of that difficult behavior. You may even want to talk to them and say that you understand that things used to be run this way, but that you plan to do things a little differently. This can help everyone relax a little because they'll have a better understanding of you and your management style.

As a new manager, you should also try to understand the inter-team dynamics that are in place. Observe how the team interacts with each other on a daily basis and how they respond to different situations. You'll soon be able to see who rubs whom the wrong way and which people don't work well together. You'll gain insight into what the team mindset is and what kind of corporate culture has been created. Once you see and understand these things, you can act on them to prevent them from causing problems that will derail your team.

CREATE RESPECT

When you come into a new management position, you need to demonstrate to your team that you will treat them with respect and set the expectation that you want them to interact with you and other members of the team and company the same way. Sometimes, this can be challenging, particularly if you have employees who think you're just another annoying boss there to ruin their lives.

Some managers come into a new job and bend over backward to be friendly and accommodating. Unfortunately, this encourages the team to take advantage of the boss and not show her true respect. Find a balance between being nice and having reasonable, enforceable expectations that create results. You can be both nice and respected by your employees. Bad apples may try to take advantage of you when you start at a new company, so you need to be aware and prepared to prevent that from happening.

Keep in mind that respect is earned over time, not all at once. While your position or title may command respect to your face, you want employees to respect you even when you're not standing in front of them. Remember that authority follows respect. Your new employees need to respect you in order for you to have any real authority over them. Bad employees will be the hardest to win over and it will take consistent effort on your part to help them develop real respect for you.

To earn the respect of a team that is new to you:

- Be consistent in the directions you provide
- Be consistent in the responses you have to situations
- Back your team when appropriate
- Demonstrate your commitment to their improvement
- Operate with honesty and integrity
- Always show respect for your individual team members and insist they respect each other

WEIGHING VALUE TO THE COMPANY

As we've mentioned in previous chapters, bad employees are determined not by how crazy they drive you, but by weighing whether their problems outweigh their value to the company. Once you are past the initial period in your role as a new manager, you'll start to form assessments of your employees and will begin to identify your bad apples. Once you've identified these employees, you should consider their problems against the backdrop of their value to the company.

Value can be hard to quantify, but consider:

- What impact the employee has on the company, both internally and externally
- The importance of the employee's role within the team
- Any ties or influence the employee has to revenue
- The amount of work the employee produces
- Ways in which the employee saves the company money
- Special skills or the level of expertise the employee has

It's important to understand value so you can begin to think about whether the bad apple is one that you should attempt to keep or consider eliminating.

TIPPING POINT

You may eventually reach a point where you want to fire an inherited employee. Sometimes, though, it's hard to know exactly when things have reached that "tipping point"—the moment when you realize that an employee is not working out, not improving, or not fulfilling her role in a reasonable way. What is the final straw that breaks the camel's back?

In most cases, if you are gradually moving toward a tipping point with an inherited employee, you need to thoughtfully consider the person's value versus the problems he causes. You don't want to act too quickly (unless you are in a sudden crisis that necessitates an immediate firing), because an employee's behavior and performance can and will fluctuate; if this is someone you don't know very well, you don't really understand what you can expect from her. You should be on the lookout for patterns of behavior that suggest that this person is more trouble than she is worth. It's also important to remember that it will take employees time to adjust to you and your management style.

apples to apples A CASE STUDY

Elizabeth works in the landscaping company office that Ashley has just been hired to manage. One of Elizabeth's roles is to schedule the trucks for topsoil deliveries. As Ashley settled into the office manager job, she noticed that Elizabeth doesn't schedule the deliveries by location—something the previous manager didn't require. With the price of gas rising, Ashley realizes the company could save a lot of money if deliveries were clustered by location. Ashley explains this to Elizabeth and suggests a method for scheduling. Elizabeth doesn't like to be told what to do and is comfortable with her old routine, so she sometimes does as she was instructed, but often "forgets" and sets the deliveries up in the order the calls come in for them. Ashley works with her to try to help her understand how to schedule by location, but doesn't make a lot of progress.

One day the drivers miss a delivery to a key client because they were at the other end of the county and couldn't get there in time. The client is very upset and threatens to find another company. If Elizabeth had clustered the deliveries by location this would never have happened. Ashley realizes that this is the tipping point for Elizabeth and decides to let her go.

ALTERNATIVES TO FIRING

When you inherit an employee who isn't fulfilling her role well, firing is just one option available to you. Firing has to be your last option though—if you started firing everyone who presented some kind of problem, you would soon be left without a team! When you take on a team with an employee who is difficult, you want to consider all your options, which include:

- **Live with it.** This might not seem like a great solution, but sometimes you have no choice. If the person can't be fired (see Chapter 1), you may well be stuck. It's almost always a good idea to try to live with the person for a while before considering termination, because there's a chance that you'll find a way to deal with the situation or to help your bad apple improve.
- **Move him to another team.** Getting someone off your team is usually just as good as firing him—then he's no longer your problem. He may fit better in another job or on another team, so this change of environment may improve his value to the company. You can encourage an employee to consider internal job postings, or recommend him to another manager (just be sure that you are truthful when you make the recommendation). This solution is particularly good when the main problem is a personality conflict with your team and the employee is actually a solid one.
- **Minimize the employee's impact.** Stop giving her important work, insulate clients and vendors from her, and reduce

her role in anything she could screw up. If she's trouble, reduce the opportunity for her to make trouble.

- **Change his behavior.** See Chapter 5 for more information about this.

Note that you might have to try several of these options before you find one that really works.

FIRING AN INHERITED EMPLOYEE

There are some special considerations when you decide you finally must fire an employee who was on your team when you were hired. If possible, talk to other managers in your company about the situation. You want to make sure that you have all the information available. For example, you may not know that the employee has gone through rough patches before, but has always managed to pull it together when told he was going to be fired if he didn't. Without knowing this history, you may just get rid of him. Knowing this however, you may be able to help him pull things together and avoid having to get rid of him and find a replacement.

If you do need to fire an inherited bad apple, it's important to talk with your team afterward (*not* before!). They will probably be concerned that you are going to clean house and start over with a whole new team. Reassure them that employees who are doing their jobs have nothing to worry about. Don't discuss the reasons you fired the person who is gone or talk negatively about her. Instead, focus your conversation on how the team as a whole is going to move forward.

CHAPTER 4

BAD APPLES OUTSIDE OF YOUR CONTROL

Every company has difficult people. It is one thing to have someone on your team who you must manage, try to rehabilitate, or work around if firing is not an option. However, it's an entirely different situation when the bad apple does not fall within your area of responsibility and authority.

CH 1. What Is a Bad Apple?

CH 2. Types of Bad Apples

CH 3. Bad Apples You Inherit

CH 4. Bad Apples Outside of Your Control

EMPLOYEES NOT UNDER YOUR SUPERVISION

Employees who work for other supervisors or who are on other teams can be challenging. Learning how to deal with them—and help your team members deal with them—takes careful consideration. When you are involved in a situation with an employee who does not work for you directly, be careful not to overstep your bounds or violate the chain of command. Keep in mind that you may not know all the details of that person's role, responsibilities, situation, or circumstances.

This kind of situation requires more tact and sensitivity on your part than dealing with people under your supervision. Remember, internal politics and other dynamics could be playing a role in the situation without it being obvious to you.

apples to apples A CASE STUDY

Lara was a manager who had a problem with Jenna, an employee on another team. Jenna had been irritable, defensive, and wasn't getting her work done on time. Unfortunately, Lara immediately escalated the situation. She was taken aback when she learned that Jenna's mother was being cared for by hospice and was in the end stage of cancer. Jenna's own manager was aware of this and had been cutting her some slack. Lara wished she had not reacted so quickly and learned that it's important to get all the facts about an employee or colleague before taking disciplinary action.

CONTACT WITH YOU

When you're the one having contact with a problem employee who is not under your supervision you may feel that there's nothing you can do to change the situation, but in fact, there's a lot you can do. You first want to try to solve the problem yourself. Think about the situation carefully and analyze what's being done that's annoying or disruptive to your work. Since you are a supervisor, you probably have some authority in his eyes, so try to work through the situation as you would if he were on your own team. Talk to him, express your concern about the situation, and ask him to make some changes. For example, suggest that David spellcheck his invoices before he sends them to your team's clients. A simple request or suggestion like this can solve the problem quickly and easily without a lot of conflict, meetings, and oversight.

If you can't get anywhere on your own, your next step is to escalate the situation and talk with the problem person's manager. However, be careful in these kinds of interactions. You don't want it to seem as if you're telling the other manager how to do his job, and criticizing one of his employees' behavior can come off that way. You also don't want to approach the other manager and dump the whole thing in his lap. Instead, *ask* for his help with this problem. Explain the steps you've taken to resolve the situation on your own and why they've apparently not worked. This way, it's clear that you're not involving the other manager unnecessarily. Emphasize that you're trying to find a solution that will work for everyone.

Before talking to the other manager, be sure you have your facts straight. You don't want to get into a "he said, she said" situation. It's also important that you be as objective as possible. You don't want to look like you're out for revenge or payback.

Understand that the other manager is probably going to be defensive and protect his own team. You most likely would be too, and that's to be expected. You need to be very insistent and clear about what the problem is. You should expect the other manager to give the situation a certain amount of weight because you are another supervisor, however, if this is a person you don't see eye to eye with, it may be a bit of a challenge.

CONTACT WITH YOUR TEAM

It's a simple fact that people within an office or a company sometimes have problems with each other; this is certainly not limited to people who are on the same team. An employee in your art department may have an ongoing issue with an employee in the technology department. Sometimes there are legitimate reasons for the conflict, other times people just rub each other the wrong way. When you have employees on two teams who have a problem with each other, sorting it out can be complicated.

You first want to find out what's going on and get your employee's side of the story. Try to pinpoint whether there is something going on that can be actively solved, such as changing some office procedure or deciding on some point of dispute the two people are having, such as whether e-mail should be logged in a client file. Keep an open mind and realize that your employee might be the bad apple in this scenario—you can't always assume that the person on the other team is at fault, although you should have some loyalty to your team that allows you to offer benefit of the doubt to some extent.

When you see a conflict brewing between one of your employees and someone on another team, try to nip it in the bud as soon as possible. If you don't, it can linger and will eventually escalate. The longer it goes on, the worse it will get. If you ask Neepa to work on a project with Kevin from another team and she rolls her eyes or exhibits negative body language, ask her if there is a problem. Find out if her concerns are with the task or the person. If there is a problem with Kevin, find out what it is and see if there's something you can do to resolve the problem.

If you can't find a solution (and many times if two people irritate each other or one of the players is a bad apple, there may not be a solution), offer your employee some advice about dealing with a difficult person, such as:

- Avoid him.
- Don't participate in arguments she starts.
- Refuse to be baited.
- Talk only about work that needs to be done.
- Avoid saying anything you know will start a tiff.
- Avoid being in direct one-on-one contact with the problem person by having someone else with you. This may deter the other person from starting trouble, and provide a witness if he does.
- Arrange to have you, the manager, nearby for an anticipated conflict.

If the problem continues, you may need to talk to the other employee's manager to let her know about the situation. It's important that when the two of you talk, you do so carefully. You want to be careful not to get in a room with the other manager and complain to each other about how annoying and childish your employees are (and this can be very tempting at times), or betray a confidence your team member has shared with you. At some level, you may have some unspoken communication about that, but you should focus your words on finding a way to end the conflict between the two employees. The simplest solution is to minimize contact between them, and this may mean agreeing to make some procedural changes. You want to protect your employee during this conversation—you have some loyalty to him, but, at the same time, be aware that he may not have told you the whole story. If something formal (such as a writeup or warning) with regard to the employee on the other team is necessary, let the other manager handle it.

Jumping the Chain of Command

Often employees jump up the chain of command when they have a complaint. Let's say you are a VP and have a supervisor, Janice, beneath you. One of Janice's team members has come to you with a complaint about another employee. When talking to the employee, find out exactly what the problem is and ask why he bypassed Janice to speak to you (there may be a potential problem with Janice that you need to know about). After you talk to the employee, you must go to Janice and get her involved—not only to discuss why she was bypassed, but also to give her a chance to handle it. It's important that you let the employee know that you're going to talk with Janice about the situation, so he's not surprised to find out she is involved. If you allow this employee to come to you and cut Janice out of the picture, you're basically telling the entire team that they don't have to follow the chain of command.

Remember, when discussing a problem that exists between people on your different teams, you want to be careful not to point the finger at the other manager or blame him for the conflict. He may report what you said back to his employee, so don't assume any sort of confidentiality in the conversation. Another important thing to remember is not to assume any confidentiality in e-mail you might send to the other manager about this. Although it is irresponsible for another manager to forward an e-mail from you to the employee in question, it happens all the time. You send Doug an e-mail about the situation between your employee Tanya and his employee Rich. He hits forward and sends it to Rich with the comment "What's going on with this?" Although this is an unacceptable and lazy management approach, you can never trust that it won't happen, so don't put anything in an e-mail that you aren't willing to let other people read.

If the other manager doesn't believe you or blows off the situation, you may have to go up the chain of command to get the situation resolved. Be sure to follow proper procedure and give the other manager every opportunity to resolve it first. If she won't, or promises to and doesn't follow through, tell her that if it isn't resolved you'll need to go up the chain of command with it. Some people feel uncomfortable escalating the situation like this, but remember that it is your job to be an advocate for your team member. If you sit back and do nothing, your team member may go to your boss with the problem and then you'll need to explain why you didn't take appropriate steps.

OTHER TEAMS

Sometimes you'll have an adversarial situation between two teams. The sales team may collectively think that the customer service team is lazy, sloppy, unfriendly, or unskilled. This kind of situation is common because people in similar jobs often have a lot of similarities, so all the members of your creative team may be liberal, artsy, and laidback, whereas an accounting team might be a bit more serious and not as flexible. When you have two groups of people who have some well-established differences, conflict isn't unusual.

Another common problem is that the two teams may have very different goals and may not see eye to eye. The sales team just wants to make sales, whereas a fulfillment team actually has to get those orders filled within a certain time frame. The sales team may not take the fulfillment team's limitations into consideration because they are just out there trying to sell as much as possible.

The company's situation can also create an adversarial feeling between teams. When a company is doing well, sins are easily forgiven, but when a company is doing poorly, the general mood of the workplace can make people likely to focus on situations they would otherwise ignore or let go. Sometimes this is a way to place blame for the company's problems. Other times it is just a result of the stress or unhappy mood of the employees in general. Either way, the higher the level of stress in your office, the more likely it is that teams will find problems with each other.

How you talk about other teams is a very important factor in how your team will react to them. It's not appropriate for you to trash-talk in front of your employees, even if you do it subtly ("We all know what they're like over in HR"). When you denigrate another team, you're implicitly giving your team permission to do so as well.

You may also experience some team-to-team conflict that starts out as a one-to-one conflict. One of your employees may have a problem with a member of a different team (who may be a classic bad apple). Over time, various employees may end up involved in different ways, until eventually it becomes a team-against-team problem. People tend to pick sides in a conflict and sometimes people on your team may actually side with the people on the other team. This will result in your group fracturing and pulling apart. If this happens, conflicts that may have been brewing on your own team can erupt into the open, further compounding the problems. Some solutions for team-to-team conflict are:

- Develop a better working relationship with the other team's manager. Cooperation trickles down.
- Recognize when a conflict is brewing and step in immediately.
- Appeal to a leader (a team member who is not necessarily in a management role, but is a key influencer on your team) within your team who can exert her influence and help the team get over whatever the problem is.
- Create an opportunity for the teams to interact in a nonwork environment, such as at a happy hour or bowling night.
- Sit them all down together, but only in the most extreme circumstances. You don't want to give the situation more importance than necessary. This can turn into gripe session if you aren't careful. If you do need to sit the two teams down to talk, you must control the situation very carefully. Any time you get a group of employees together to discuss something, it's helpful to set expectations for the meeting. Tell them why you're having it and what you hope to get out of it. This prevents it from veering out of your control.
- Switch roles for a day. Have your team work or observe the other team's jobs for one day or just a few hours and vice versa. Everyone will come away with a better understanding of the responsibilities that each job involves.

OTHER SUPERVISORS

Supervisors are people, too, and some have annoying quirks, personality problems, or don't work well in an environment that involves other teams. And, of course, a supervisor can be a bad apple, too. A conflict with another supervisor can be tense for everyone involved.

SUPERVISORS AT YOUR LEVEL

The other supervisors in your company who are on the same level as you may be great colleagues, but sometimes you'll run across one and scratch your head, wondering how on earth he got where he is. It can be hard to decide what to do in this situation. You may feel as if you don't want to stick your nose into other people's situations, but you have an obligation to your company to get everyone to perform at their best level. Because of this, it probably isn't appropriate to let someone who is doing a terrible job continue to do so, even if he is another supervisor.

The caveat here of course is you don't know what that person's situation is, whether his manager is working with him on improvement, or what exactly may have transpired. Be sensitive to these possibilities. Sometimes the best solution is to talk to the person and find out what's going on. If he's struggling with something, you may be able to help. If this supervisor is newer to the company, you could offer to mentor him. You must be careful not to be condescending if you offer this.

If the other supervisor's actions or behavior are having a big impact on your company's business, you've noticed an ongoing pattern of problems, and there seems to be nothing you can do to help him, you need to make sure that your concerns are sent up the chain of command. While it's tempting to say, "I'm not involved," and turn a blind eye, a good manager always has the best interests of the company at heart. If this person is truly a bad apple, upper management will make the decision to keep him or let him go. If you or the other manager are new to the job, don't overreact. Allow things time to calm down before you do anything. Remember, anything new that happens in a company can cause ripples.

It can be hard to make the decision to take action about another manager's performance. If you are the program manager for client training and you hear through the grapevine that the purchasing manager's approach with vendors is causing them to return higher bids, which is creating more expense for your company, you may think this has nothing to do with you and consider forgetting about it. However, if the situation continues, it could influence the company's bottom line, which means you need to get involved.

Once you've made the decision to escalate, decide who to talk to. If you have a shared boss (you're both directly under the CIO, for example), go to that boss. If you are in different divisions, it makes sense to go to your boss and explain the situation. Your boss can then talk to the boss of the problem manager.

Even though letting a problem with another manager ride may negatively influence the company in a serious way, a lot of managers fear getting involved because they worry that speaking up will either permanently damage their relationship with the bad manager or that it will damage their own reputation within the company. Sometimes you can't avoid hurting someone, but if you want to be a successful manager, you have to put your company first. If your relationship is damaged, you will have to deal with it, but it's likely that a manager that bad isn't going to last long with the company. And, while some people may decide you're a backstabber, chances are that there are going to be a lot of people who are grateful you pointed out the problem.

MANAGERS ABOVE YOU

Many managers have been in the position of having a boss or a higher-up in the company who is a complete jerk. Unfortunately, bad apples can exist at any level in a company. When your own boss is hard to work for, you need to work out some strategies to keep your sanity and keep your job.

The first thing to do is cover your behind! Protect yourself so you can keep your job. If this manager is incompetent or is someone with whom you do not get along, you want to make sure you're not thrown under the bus. Be sure your work gets done and that you keep notes that indicate the instructions you were given whenever possible.

Don't assume your manager is being a jerk on purpose. If there's something she's doing that bothers you, talk to her! She may not realize she's doing it or even have any idea that people are bothered by it. It's always a good idea to keep the lines of communication open and to share your concerns with your manager.

If you have a true bad apple for a boss, do some mental calculations. How long is he going to last in this position? How long will you be there? Can you tolerate the situation for that long? If yes, keep your mouth shut and deal with it. If it looks like both of you are there for the long run, then you need to think about your alternatives. You have a few choices:

- **Get out.** Ask for a transfer within the company or apply for another position within the company.
- **Minimize contact.** If you plan to stay in your job, see what you can do to minimize your dealings with him.
- **Go over his head.** If you're not going to be able to stand the situation and you can't leave, this option allows you to go to a higher-up and present your concerns.

If you decide to go over your boss's head, make sure you don't appear to be backstabbing. You don't want to get a reputation as the person who always complains about people to his boss. If you are the marketing manager and your boss, the VP of sales and marketing, is a complete jerk who makes it impossible for you to do your job, go to the CEO and frame the situation in a way that does not appear to be backstabbing. Say: "I don't know how to handle this situation. I need some help."

If you can't use any of these three strategies, you need to find other ways to maintain your sanity:

- Change your mindset and accept the situation for what it is. Stop fretting and fighting things you have no control over. Focus on what you can control and let the rest go.
- Develop a long-term strategy to move to another company so you have constructive things you can do to eventually change your situation. Brush up your resume, make contacts, take a class that will further your qualifications, etc.
- Find ways to relieve the stress. Take up a hobby, exercise, get enough sleep, and find distractions that take your mind off the bad situation at work. If you don't, you'll find that the stress will interfere with all aspects of your life.

CORPORATE CULTURE

Your company's corporate culture can also be responsible for creating bad apples throughout the organization. It's important to differentiate between corporate culture and corporate climate. Corporate climate has to do with the facts of business for your company and can include:

- Unemployment rates
- Lawsuits against the company
- Layoffs
- The economic state of the region, state, or country
- New corporate acquisitions
- Employee benefits
- Hiring freezes

- Wage freezes
- Mandatory overtime
- New management
- Profit sharing
- Bonuses

These are major business events that create a climate for your company. This climate influences how employees feel, which is the corporate culture. If the climate is negative (layoffs, uncertainty about benefits, or wage freezes), the corporate culture is going to react to that, with people becoming self-protective and less willing to invest time and energy in the company. If the climate is positive, the corporate culture reflects that as well, with a more relaxed workplace and employees who are excited to contribute.

When the corporate climate is negative, the corporate culture is going to become a breeding ground for difficult employee behavior. More and more people are going to exhibit bad apple behavior, and some employees are going to morph into true bad apples.

As a manager, you may have limited ability to have an impact on the climate, but you can have an effect on the people who are reacting to the climate, at least within your own team (and one team's attitude has a way of affecting other team's attitudes, so if you can implement some change to the culture, you will see it spread). If the corporate culture is evolving into something you don't see as positive, create a subculture for your team. Do things that improve the working atmosphere, such as dress-down Fridays, joke of the day e-mail (remember to be extremely sensitive to any potential offensive content), or DJ of the day (employees take turns playing their office-appropriate playlists). Be aware that your tone and demeanor has a huge impact on that of your team. If you're down and worried, your employees will be, too. If you are cheerful and pleasant, it will rub off.

You can also have an impact on your team by keeping it focused on positive things. Announce big sales or successfully launched projects that you wouldn't make a big deal of in a good climate. Unless your company is going out of business, there are positive things you can emphasize to your team. To have an impact on the overall corporate culture:

- Try to develop and foster an attitude among management that sees workers as people, not just bodies filling jobs. You need to implement an attitude of respect that becomes pervasive throughout the company.
- Provide for interaction among employees whenever possible. People who are nose down to the computer for eight hours straight are not going to be very happy employees.
- Make work fun when possible. A little humor goes a long way toward changing people's attitudes and perceptions about their jobs and company.
- Take a collaborative approach when possible. Employees who work together feel more positive about their jobs and workplace.
- Implement mentoring programs. When people help other people, everyone benefits and walks away feeling more positive.

The corporate culture can be influenced and this can help keep bad apple behavior to a minimum.

PART 2

PROBLEM-**SOLVING**
TECHNIQUES

CHAPTER 5

MOTIVATING BAD APPLES TO BECOME GOOD

It's almost always easier to improve a bad employee than to go through the hiring and firing process. And if you have an employee whom you can't fire—or who would be very difficult to fire—finding a way to improve what you've got may be your only option.

It is absolutely untrue that difficult employees cannot be turned around. It's very possible to motivate an employee to have a change in attitude, work habits, and output. The key is understanding what kind of motivation to use and how to implement it.

CH 5. Motivating Bad Apples to Become Good

CH 6. Maintaining Good Apples

CH 7. Dealing with Personality Conflicts

CH 8. Cultivating Conflict Resolution Skills

CH 9. Disciplining Bad Apples

CH 10. Ditching Bad Apples

CH 11. Considering Legal Ramifications

IDENTIFY THE PROBLEM

Before you can create a solution, you need to understand what's wrong. While there may be some clearly identifiable problems with an employee, spend some time thinking about the full scope of the problem.

apples to apples A CASE STUDY

Deena works for Maria in a shipping company. It kept coming to Maria's attention that Deena often had incorrect pricing on her reports, but Maria didn't realize why this was happening until she took the time to sit down and talk with Deena. It turned out that Deena was using an old pricing sheet; in fact, she always failed to update this type of information in her reference material. If Maria hadn't taken the time to discover the reason behind the problem, she may have just reprimanded Deena and asked her to use the correct pricing. In which case, Deena may have fixed that problem, but may have also continued to use other outdated materials.

To identify the full scope of a problem:

- Talk to the employee. Ask questions and have a real conversation about what's going wrong. Ask about related areas as well.
- Try to get a sense from the rest of the team as to what's happening. Often they know exactly what's going on.
- Be an observer. If you take some time to just sit with your team, watch them handle projects, and float around the center of activity, you will pick up a lot of information

and be able to see how well they're working and exactly what is going on.

Being a careful observer may help you realize that there are things going on that you weren't aware of, such as the fact that the company hasn't raised wages in three years, key employees were lost and not replaced, or bad employees have been kept, which has affected the entire team.

When you realize you have an employee who is difficult, it is helpful to identify what type of bad apple he really is (see Chapter 2). Being able to categorize the person makes it easier to create solutions and focus in on the behavior you want to change.

UNDERSTAND THE CAUSATION

Once you fully understand exactly what the employee is doing wrong, take some time to understand what has caused this behavior to happen. Sometimes it's as simple as realizing that the employee is not skilled or experienced enough to handle the job. Other times, it can be much more complex. There could be something in the work environment or job responsibilities that is causing your employee to behave this way. She could be experiencing a personality conflict with someone else in the office. Also, some people have personalities that make them incompatible with certain jobs or responsibilities. It's also possible that a combination of factors is causing the problem.

It's important to remember that every behavior a person exhibits is motivated by something. They are either acting out emotions, taking action to achieve a certain outcome, or have deeply ingrained habits or traits they are unable to control. You need to identify the motivating factor, because that is the thing you want to take charge of or change. It sounds sort of controlling (like you're going to achieve total mind control over your assistant somehow), but it's simple human psychology. To work effectively with people, you have to understand what makes them tick.

Look objectively at the problem behavior and think about why the employee is doing it. What could possibly make someone think that this is the way to behave? What does he see himself as getting from it? What benefits does it offer him?

If you can pinpoint the benefits the behavior provides her, then you are in a position to substitute similar benefits that she will realize if she adopts the behavior you want her to. So if Lynnette is a poisoner who turns your team against every project or change, you need to think about what she gains from doing that. It may be that doing this gives her a feeling of control in an environment in which she feels out of control. If you can see that, you can think of ways to give Lynnette a feeling of control without allowing her to poison things. Give her responsibilities or let her be the decision-maker on some tasks.

DEMONSTRATE THE BENEFITS OF BEING A GOOD APPLE

One of the easiest ways to motivate an employee to improve is to have a reward in front of him that he will receive if he reaches certain goals. Show him what the benefits and rewards are for good job performance. These can include:

- Compliments and public recognition (including things like certificates, "employee of the month," or small prizes)
- Promotions
- Merit raises
- Enhanced responsibility

- Additional benefits (such as the ability to work on flex time, an additional personal day, etc.)
- Paid training or classes to further his qualifications and skills (which could lead to promotions or raises)

Many managers don't optimize these rewards enough. It's one thing to know you can offer them, but it is another thing entirely to make sure your employees know what they are. You've got to talk about them instead of allowing them to be mysterious vague possibilities. It can also be helpful to make rewards more accessible. If you tell your team they will all get raises if they increase sales by $2 million this year, that goal can seem too hard to achieve. If you tell them they will get to leave early on Fridays for the month of August if they meet a certain sales goal for the month of June, then you've offered something that is much more attainable and possible.

If you offer small, incremental rewards, your bad employee will be more likely to get on the ladder to success than if you tell him he's got to fly like Superman and surpass a huge challenge. All employees can benefit from a gradual reward system, but difficult employees in particular will be motivated by this because you are able to slowly steer them toward good behavior, almost without them realizing what you are doing.

CONSEQUENCES

Rewards are an important part of getting bad employees on track, but you also must know how to use consequences effectively. Some employees are more easily motivated by fear or things that would be detrimental to them than by the idea of a promotion or an employee parking spot. There can be many consequences you can use, such as:

- Termination
- Demotion
- Losing privileges
- Removal from projects or loss of responsibility
- "Writing up" (formal recording of the problem in the employee's record)
- Public embarrassment (like calling someone out in front of his peers)

As with rewards, these consequences will be more motivating to some employees than they will be to others. For example, if Shane is your lazy employee and you have to have a talk with him about how he slacked off and did not complete the programming on a website he was working on, threatening to reduce the number of projects he is working on may not be an outcome he sees as negative. Be sure to tailor your possible consequences to the employee.

Never make threats you are not prepared or able to carry out. If you do, your employees will learn that you don't have the follow-through to make anything stick. They need to completely believe everything you tell them.

DEALING WITH YOUR OWN FEELINGS

Some managers are uncomfortable sitting face to face with an employee and telling him he's doing a bad job. You might worry about hurting his feelings, be concerned he will quit, or feel like a jerk sitting there criticizing someone else. The fact is, pointing out concerns and offering methods for improvement are part of your job as a manager. You're there to keep your team working smoothly. If something is going wrong, it's your responsibility to step in and create change.

Here are a few things to keep in mind that will make things more comfortable for you:

- Employees usually welcome input. No, nobody likes to be told they're not doing a good job, but most people would rather you told them what they were doing wrong and offer them suggestions than leave them to mess things up on their own.
- Your employee wants to keep her job. This is a huge motivating factor for her, so she's going to at least try to be receptive to your suggestions and critique.
- It's possible to offer criticism without being mean. There are a lot of ways to convey your thoughts to your employee without making him feel bad. Criticism doesn't have to be "you're a stupid jerk and need to shape up." A good manager can find reassuring and positive ways to help employees improve what they're doing. If you genuinely feel you are trying to help that person, it changes the dynamic of the conversation and makes it less uncomfortable for you.
- If an employee is not performing well, it will reflect badly on you. Helping her improve will further your own career.
- Your employees expect their boss to actively supervise them. If you sit in your ivory tower and never show your face, your employees are going to feel disconnected from you.
- You have nothing to apologize for. Offering critiques and suggestions is part of your job.

No matter what you do, every time you have to talk with an employee about a problem, there is going to be tension—it's simply the nature of the interaction. You need to learn to be comfortable in your role. If you can have these kinds of talks without working yourself up into a sweat beforehand, they will be more comfortable for everyone involved.

HOW TO TALK ABOUT THE PROBLEM

Many times you will be able to have casual conversations with employees about problems that have happened or improvements that need to be made. You may pass by Alex's desk and stop to ask him to make some changes to a report. Bad apples won't respond to these casual encounters as readily. They force you to have a more formal approach. However, when you're dealing with a bad apple, it's more likely the problems you're attempting to address are bigger, longer term, and more difficult to solve, so it probably necessitates a serious conversation in your office or other private area.

Take a few minutes before your meeting to think through what your main points are. You may want to discuss the following:

- What the problem is
- Why the problem needs to be solved or improved on (such as the impact it is having on the team or company)
- Ideas you've come up with that will help bring about change
- How the employee thinks things could be changed or improved (giving her a voice in the solution makes it more likely she will actually follow through on the plan)
- What the time frame is for the plan you're working out

When you start to have the conversation, outline the point of the talk. Explain that there's a problem you're going to talk about and then you'll discuss strategies together. Say that you hope to improve the situation for both of you. Laying out the general outline of the conversation will help put the employee at ease and he will know what to expect. If you don't give some explanation at the beginning, it's likely your employee is going to sit there thinking "Oh my gosh, is she going to fire me? What am I going to do if she fires me?" She won't be able to concentrate on the conversation and a lot of what you say will be lost.

HAVE AN EFFECTIVE CONVERSATION

When you need to talk with a bad apple about a concern or problem, be sure to focus on your goal. Bad employees in particular may try to change the topic, bring up their own concerns, throw blame on others, and do other things to dodge and weave throughout the conversation. Remind yourself that the reason you're having the conversation is to achieve a certain outcome, such as changing his behavior, making sure he understands consequences, or to get more respect.

An effective conversation will paint a picture of an outcome that is win-win. Both you and the employee will gain something or benefit from the outcome that you are trying to implement. A conversation that sets up an outcome that only benefits you is unlikely to motivate your difficult employee to make any changes at all.

If you have a slob on your team who doesn't dress professionally, but is always bugging you to put him on bigger projects, you need to explain to him that you've been hesitant to assign him to those projects because you don't think the clients will view him as professional. If he changes the way he presents himself, you are willing to place him on larger projects. You've offered him a win-win situation. He gets opportunities that will further his career and could lead to promotions, income, or other positive benefits for him. You win because the company gets to put a good employee on important accounts. If you had this same conversation, but did not present the benefits to him, he would have no reason to change the way he dresses.

During your conversation, show some level of appreciation for how the person feels or the situation he is in. Genuine empathy cannot be underrated. If you make it clear that you understand where he is coming from, he's more likely to want to understand where you're coming from.

Present the outcome of your discussion as "our solution" instead of "my solution" whenever possible. Make it clear that you are vested in the employee's career and want him to succeed (even if you secretly hate him). Frame your solution so that the employee sees it as something you're going to work toward together. If you sit him down, tell him he's doing a crummy job, then put all the responsibility for changing the situation on his shoulders, it's unlikely he is going to succeed. You want to make sure he knows that you're going to be there to help him along.

When you talk to your bad apple about the problem and possible solutions, here are some things you definitely should avoid:

- **Avoid confrontation.** A discussion between a manager and employee should never become a confrontation pitting one person against the other. There is nothing in that dynamic that will help improve the situation. Instead, keep in mind that you are both really on the same side. You want this employee to succeed and she wants the same thing.
- **Never get into a shouting match.** You're the one directing the conversation and controlling the tone, so you're the one who must prevent this. If the employee you are talking to gets angry and raises his voice, remember that people

will stop shouting if you don't shout back. The louder he gets, the quieter you get. It is often not helpful to say, "Calm down," because this makes the person think you are not taking his concerns seriously.

- **Don't be afraid of silence.** If you feel like things are escalating or becoming confusing, take a deep breath and a moment to gather your thoughts.
- **Keep your annoyance to yourself.** Sometimes it can be useful to let someone know how much they have annoyed you or made your life difficult, but in most situations it just muddies the waters. Treat the employee with respect and the conversation will be much smoother.
- **Avoid referencing other employees as much as possible.** You don't want to say, "Well, Amy seems to be able to handle this amount of work. I don't know why you can't."
- **Don't set unrealistic requirements.** Goals and challenges should be within your employee's ability.
- **Give your employee room to speak.** Refusing to let your employee offer an explanation will cause resentment, so allow him some time to account for his bad apple behavior.

DEALING WITH RESPONSES

There three main types of responses you can get when you talk with an employee about making a change or improvement:

- The employee agrees too readily and doesn't hear what you're saying. She's overly anxious to please you and will say anything to solve the problem.
- He fights everything you say and offers explanations and excuses. He may ultimately agree to try to work on the things you've suggested, but doesn't really intend to.

- She thinks over what you say and asks thoughtful questions. Whether she agrees with what you've said or not, she does agree to try to work toward the solution with genuine effort.

In the first two situations, you can take some steps to help the employee really understand what you're after. Ask her to explain what she will do differently in the future to avoid the problem you are discussing. This forces her to internalize what you've said and rephrase it. This mental process makes it more likely the employee will actually make the effort you're asking for.

Another way to ensure the employee will follow through is to present the problem then ask him what he thinks he can do. If you've got a waster who is using too many resources, ask him what solutions he can come up with that will reduce his resource use. When you involve the employee in creating the solution, he is more likely to carry through on it.

WORDS THAT WORK

You might be unsure about how to phrase what you need to say to your employee. Here are some suggestions:

- I'd like to see some improvement with X.
- We need you to get to the point where you're producing Y.
- Your work on A hasn't been where we need it to be and here's why. Let's work out a plan for how you're going to improve that.
- I'm concerned because I see that you're doing this and this.
- I understand how you feel, but I've been tracking your work on this and you can see that on these dates such and such happened. It is a pattern and one we need to work on.
- Our goal here is to find a way to improve the situation.

A PLAN FOR IMPROVEMENT

Your employee isn't going to improve if you just tell her to pull it together. She needs specific guidelines and instructions about what she can do to improve. The clearer you can spell it out for her, the easier it will be for her to meet your expectations.

Your plan should be made up of tangible actions that you both agree to. It needs to be concrete and easy to follow. Vague agreements to "do better" or "improve" are nebulous and not very helpful. Instead, create a step-by-step process that the employee can easily follow. It is also essential that the plan you put in place is attainable. If you set your expectations too high, your employee will fail before she begins.

If you are dealing with a serious situation that requires you to record the incident and the agreed-upon solution in the employee's file, make sure that the file reflects the steps the employee is required to take and impose a timeline. It's not enough to say that Michelle will learn to operate the postage meter correctly; you need to say she will master it by next week. If the problem does not merit a formal note to the personnel file, then at least be sure to follow up the talk with an e-mail that outlines the steps you agreed to. Having a plan in writing makes it easier to follow and prevents the possibility that the employee can say she misunderstood what you were asking for later.

You also need to create a private plan for yourself, so you have an idea of how often to monitor the employee and what benchmarks are you are looking for. You need to know what kind of assistance you're going to offer and how you're going to be there to help shepherd the employee toward the goal. Again, the solution must be one that you will work toward together, so it's important that you see yourself as an active participant.

AN EMPLOYEE WHO DISAGREES

Sometimes, when you talk with an employee about the problems you see, he will completely disagree with you. "I didn't forget to attach the company profiles to those e-mails. I know I put them on. Someone else must have taken it off." "I think that Jennifer and I get along just fine. She's never complained to me about my workspace being messy."

Between a Rock and a Hard Place

If your employee won't listen to your critique, refuses to participate in a plan for improvement, or makes no progress toward change, you've got to get rid of her. This is why it is so important to document everything you do, so you have evidence that you asked her for improvements, showed her what she needed to do, and can demonstrate she failed to do so.

He's entitled to his opinion and you're entitled to yours, but in the workplace, your opinion trumps his. If you think something is not working or is a problem, then it is, even if he's unwilling to see or admit it. You don't need to get him to admit to making the mistake or having the personality defect, you just need to get him to agree to take the steps that you outline. Some people will never admit that they're wrong, no matter what you do, and it's a complete waste of your time to discuss it over and over with them. Set up the plan (with his input when possible) and tell him you want him to follow it.

Remember, you don't want the conversation to devolve into an argument. You don't need an admission, you just need a willingness to try what you're suggesting. You should try to genuinely listen and acknowledge it if he makes a valid point. Don't be so rigid that you can't accept anything he says. You can prevent it from becoming a challenge by being completely prepared for the conversation. Be ready with specific examples and a clear goal in your mind for where you want to lead the meeting.

FOLLOW THROUGH

Putting a plan in place is a great way to effect some change with your difficult employee, but, by itself, a plan is not enough. You've got to follow through on monitoring, offering rewards, and providing additional suggestions and input. Too many managers work hard to put a plan in place, but then drop the ball, never following up or making sure that the plan is carried through.

Your role as a manager is to make the plan as easy as possible to follow. Make sure the plan has reasonable requirements that are easily measurable so that the employee has the opportunity for long-term success.

Schedule periodic plan reviews. Don't let them get pushed aside by other more important things on your calendar. The problem has developed over a long period of time and is not going to improve overnight. You need to be prepared to work toward a solution for the long haul. If the situation was important enough to put the plan in place, then it is important enough to follow through on.

You need to do more than just watch and wait. Acknowledge when things are going well—positive feedback will keep your employee on track and help her feel motivated to keep working. Constant reinforcement will let her know that you reward improvement and that it's possible to make a difference. Make sure she is aware that you are tracking her progress. Review the plan and its success and failure on a regular basis. The frequency of how often you look at it depends on the situation and the plan.

Sometimes as time passes, you may realize that some adjustments need to be made to the plan you've created. When you need to make adjustments, it is always better to make small changes as the situation evolves. You should only scrap the plan if you are not achieving any tangible results. However, this doesn't mean you should give up on the employee. You may find another approach that works better for that particular employee.

Employees Who Come to You

You should always be receptive to employees coming to you to talk about concerns they have. Sometimes your bad apple will open a door to a conversation by complaining or asking why he has not been promoted, given a raise, or offered certain projects. This is an excellent opening for you to talk about the problems with his work or attitude. Give him reasons someone else was chosen over him or he hasn't gotten a raise. When an employee is motivated to come to you in a situation like this, he will be more motivated to listen to what you have to say than if you go to him to start the discussion. You're more likely to get him to that "a-ha moment" in which he realizes changes are necessary.

MOTIVATING BAD APPLES IN GENERAL

Sometimes you're trying to get a bad apple over a bump in the road and moving forward. Other times, you have bad apples on your team who aren't creating any kind of urgent situation. Instead, they're just there with all of their lovely personality flaws, making things difficult or bothering people. As a manager, you should try to find a way to motivate these employees to do good work, be productive, and be generally pleasant to others.

One of the best ways to keep troublesome people moving in a positive direction is to create a friendly and pleasant work environment. (Read more about this in Chapter 7.) Encourage your employees to respect themselves. This is the foundation of workplace respect. Once employees know that you want them to respect themselves, they can move on to respecting you and their coworkers.

As the boss, make sure that you understand each employee's value and know the importance of the work they do. When your team feels understood and valued, they are more likely to perform for you. Show them that what they do and how they perform matters.

Look for times and situations where you can back off the throttle a little and take the stress out of the environment. A workplace that is really tense and rushed can definitely contribute to the way an employee feels and behaves. If you can decrease the stress, you're more likely to have employees who are happier people—and you're more likely to hold on to the good apples on your team.

CHAPTER 6

MAINTAINING GOOD APPLES

Good apples are the foundation of your team. You rely on these people; they are the employees who get the job done. The bad apples on your team can have an effect on how the solid employees perform. You shouldn't just assume that the good employees are fine and ignore them. They need your attention, particularly when there are team members who are underperforming.

CH 5. Motivating Bad Apples to Become Good

CH 6. Maintaining Good Apples

CH 7. Dealing with Personality Conflicts

CH 8. Cultivating Conflict Resolution Skills

CH 9. Disciplining Bad Apples

CH 10. Ditching Bad Apples

CH 11. Considering Legal Ramifications

THE EFFECT OF BAD APPLES ON GOOD APPLES

The saying "a bad apple will spoil the bunch" is especially true in the workplace. When you have a troublesome employee, the bad vibes can reach out and touch every member of the team. One person's dissatisfaction, bad attitude, or lack of productivity can influence everyone else in the environment, even employees who aren't in direct contact with the bad apple. You may (and should!) worry that this will lead to other employees leaving. This is a real concern, but one that you can take steps to prevent.

Remember, managing bad apples is not just about working with the challenges of the negative employees themselves, it's about helping the rest of your team work around, ignore, overcome, and cope with the negative element.

HOW A BAD APPLE INFLUENCES YOUR GOOD EMPLOYEES

This situation is more common than you might think. A study from the University of Washington, printed in *Research in Organizational Behavior*, found that bad apples in the workplace have the power to upset the whole apple cart. Teams in this situation were more likely to have conflict, poor communication, and less cooperation. The study found that team members react to the negative employee in three main ways:

- **Motivational intervention:** Talking to the individual and asking him or her to change
- **Rejection:** Asking that the bad apple be removed
- **Defensiveness:** Denial, social withdrawal, anger, anxiety, and fear

If you are managing a negative employee, it's important that you understand and anticipate these reactions and take proactive steps to quell the influence of the difficult employee on the rest of your team. Let's first think about the reactions you can expect to see from your team.

Motivational Intervention

Respond positively to motivational intervention when you see it in your team. "Jo, it was great that you recognized what a great job Mac did on the last task. I know you find him hard to work with, and this is a great way for you to help him get on track." Encourage your team to help and assist each other. The best teams find motivation from within themselves, not from an outside source, such as a supervisor. Setting up mentoring (both officially and unofficially) is another effective way to help your team build its own motivational attitude. You can assign more experienced team members to partner with less experienced members and offer them advice. You could set up a mentoring lunch once a month to allow everyone on the team to get together with their mentoring partner.

Rejection

If Ray comes to you to say that Shelly is always taking credit for his work and he no longer wants to work with her, it's important that you pay attention and respond to his concerns. Ray has to feel that you've heard him. Keep in mind that, while your team may be rejecting the negative employee, your job as a manager is to restore cohesion whenever possible. You need to find a way to help Ray and Shelly work together in a cooperative manner. This may mean changing work assignments or handling the problem by working with Shelly. If that bad apple isn't going anywhere, help your team find a way to work around her or to gradually slide that bad apple back into the heart of the team.

Defensiveness

When your team members react defensively to the negative employee, your managerial role is to help them find ways to have a positive impact on the situation. Your responsibility is also to restore order, build team morale, honor individual achievement, and take steps to make the work environment a positive place.

IMPACT ON PRODUCTIVITY

It is important that you understand the impact a challenging employee can have on your productivity. In most cases, this is obvious—if the bad apple is not doing his job, productivity is going to suffer.

Difficult employees create distraction and other members of the team will expend energy overcoming the situation instead of handling their own responsibilities. For example, Shawn's job is to count the brake pads in each box that rolls off the line. Jane packages the pads, but doesn't always put them in the box the right way. Because of this, Shawn often has to realign the pads inside the box before counting them. It takes him longer and he's more prone to make mistakes on the count since he's distracted by having to rebox the pads. Jane's poor performance decreases Shawn's productivity.

SIGNS THAT A BAD APPLE'S INFLUENCE IS SPREADING

A bad apple can quickly cause good employees to feel overburdened, become dissatisfied with you and/or the company, and either move on or become complacent. Be sure to watch for signs of this happening so you can step in and undo the damage before the bad apple's influence spreads through the whole team like a virus.

Other signs that a bad apple is having a negative impact on a good apple:

- Attitude change
- Decrease in participation or contributions at meetings (for example the employee used to ask questions, but now just sits and nods)
- Job performance suffers
- Productivity decreases
- Response to workplace stress changes
- Comments from other employees about his or her change in attitude or performance
- Others defend the bad apple's poor performance or attitude

Another situation to watch for is a good employee spending more time with a bad employee than in the past. This can be a good thing—if the influence of the good is rubbing off on the bad. But it can go the other way just as easily. While you can't and shouldn't stop coworkers from bonding, it's appropriate to monitor the situation. A general reminder (i.e., an e-mail sent to everyone as a reminder about company policy) can help influence the situation, especially if the good employee responded to this type of reminder in the past. If it doesn't work, you may need to engage in a direct, private conversation with the good employee to express your concerns.

RESPOND QUICKLY

If you sense that a good apple is beginning to go bad, it's important to act quickly and intervene before the bad habits or behavior become ingrained. The sooner you can offer constructive criticism and direction, the more likely it is that you'll be able to turn the situation around.

However, while it's a good idea to respond quickly to any changes or problems you see, you need to do so in context. If your previously reliable employee Jeremy has made several mistakes today and you come down on him like a ton of bricks with written warnings and changes to his job responsibilities, you'll do more damage than good. Respond in a way that's appropriate for the situation. In Jeremy's situation, begin by expressing concern and offering to help him.

To respond appropriately you need to find out what is causing the sudden change in behavior or performance. If you see a pattern developing, touch base with your employee and try to find what has caused the change. It doesn't do you any good to treat only the behavior—you need to determine the underlying cause.

apples to apples A CASE STUDY

Linda and Rob are members of the same team and Linda is a bad apple. She has a bad attitude about her job and rubs people the wrong way with her comments. Recently, Linda and Rob have been spending more time together. They're often seen together in the lunchroom and stop by to chat with each other often during the day. Rob was usually a punctual employee, but now he has started to arrive late with only cursory excuses. His tasks used to be done in good spirits with extra steps, creating exceptional work. Now they are done to the letter—nothing more. In a situation like this, don't sit idly by. Talk with your good apple. Ask open questions to start, such as "I've noticed you've been having trouble getting here on time lately. That doesn't seem like you. Has something changed?" Let him attempt to tell you why first. Don't mention the bad apple because, if you make that suggestion, your employee may agree with you because it's easier to do so or if he thinks that is what you wanted to hear.

TALKING ABOUT BAD APPLES

When talking to other employees about problem individuals, remember that anything you say can and will be repeated, so it's not appropriate for you to be overly candid. Some managers shy away from doing these discussions, but being unrealistic does nothing except demonstrate your failure to see and understand the frustrations of the people you're managing.

REINFORCE VALUE

If you decided (or are forced) to keep a bad apple on board, make sure that your other employees come to understand the value that bad apple brings to the company or team. Reinforce the positive attributes of that person—the skills, contacts, knowledge, or experience he or she brings to the team and to the company. Make it clear that everyone brings different things to the team and everyone has individual value. Also, let the team know that bumps in the road are to be expected, but that those won't have an impact on the long-term success you're envisioning.

apples to apples A CASE STUDY

Janice was the publisher of a small regional magazine. Her team included Kyle, a difficult advertising manager who was inconsiderate to the others, but turned out great sales numbers.

The rest of the team was uncomfortable and Janice knew she needed to do something quickly to improve the mood in the office. She began to make a point of letting each employee know how important he or she was. She told Micayla that the great content she wrote was a big reason their readership was increasing and let her know she thought that soon they would increase the size of the magazine, which would make room for more of the features that Micayla liked to write. She let the whole team know that her plan was to eventually publish every month instead of every other month and that they were all going to be an important part of that plan. The team responded well to her plans and soon saw that Kyle was an integral part of the plan for the magazine—more sales meant more success and better opportunities for all of them.

STRESS STEPS BEING TAKEN

If an employee comes to you with a complaint about a bad apple, make it clear that you (or the company) are taking steps to manage, improve, or change the problem element. You don't report to your employees, so you don't need to lay out your plans, but it's a good idea to simply say, "I know that it's frustrating that Tad has no computer skills and that it means the rest of the department has more work. We're sending him for some training, which will help improve the situation." It's also important to point out circumstances the employees may not be aware of. "It may seem like Tad is working fewer hours than you, but in fact he's been working from home every weekend and I'm pleased with his progress so far." If you can point to tangible examples of improvement and progress, do so at every opportunity. Your team will then see that change is occurring.

BE MINDFUL WHEN IN A GROUP

In most circumstances, it will not help you to embarrass employees in front of the group (although there are times when a calculated use of public embarrassment can work to your advantage). Peer pressure is already at work for you. Everyone on the team wants everyone else to do their job well so the team can succeed. Pointing a public finger at a weak link will not help matters. The difficult employee will respond negatively and your public comments will make your team feel as though it's somehow all right to be unpleasant to the employee in question. If the situation requires offering criticism in front of the group, make sure it's specific to a task or incident and not about overall performance. For example, if Emme, your receptionist, breaks the fax machine again, don't scream, "I can't believe you made the same mistake again! You're so stupid!" Instead, say, "From now on instead of loading this way, why don't you try loading it that way?" If you're really mad at Emme, express it when she's in your office with the door shut, not while she's in public. Use mistakes to help your team as a whole learn how it can do better.

DON'T ALLOW AUTOMATIC SCAPEGOATS

Bad apples can serve as easy and convenient scapegoats for good apples, so be sure to have your facts before reacting. Whether intentional or simply habit, good employees may find themselves always looking for ways in which the bad employee let the team down.

apples to apples A CASE STUDY

Kayt managed the alumni office at a college. Miranda was known among the staff as a fairly lazy employee. Instead of filing things, she would just stack them on top of the file cabinet and, instead of writing down a phone message, she would try to remember to tell the person about the call. Soon, if something was missing or some piece of information didn't get communicated, the rest of the staff would automatically blame Miranda. "I'm sorry, Kayt. I can't find the file on the reunion. I'm sure Miranda just left it somewhere." Kayt got tired of this and began to require that people check files out. She soon discovered that Miranda was not the only one misplacing things. With this information, she was able to talk with the team about the problem and deflect the blame that was unfairly placed on Miranda.

MAINTAINING GOOD APPLES

Good apples need attention, too. If you spend all of your time working through your troublesome team members' issues, you'll find that your good employees may start to drift. They need positive feedback, ongoing interaction, and reassurance.

MAKE CONNECTIONS

Staying in touch with your employees is a key way to ensure they want to stay. Good apples care about what happens to the company and their coworkers. If they see you as unaware or unresponsive, they may lose interest in the company's or team's success.

Use these methods to keep in touch with your team:

- **Be visible.** Don't sit in your office all day. Get out there and talk to them.
- **Provide opportunities for your employees to talk with you individually and as a group.** Designate times during the day or week when you are available to them.

- **Offer input without being asked.** Your role is to oversee the work your team does. Let them know you're doing that, and that you are very personally involved in the work they are doing.
- **Make it clear that you're aware of the problems they are facing.** If they know that you're in the know, they'll feel more comfortable.
- **Deal proactively with their concerns.** Don't wait for an employee to come to you to complain about the outdated fax machine. Let the team know it's in the budget to replace next year.
- **Get to know them.** Be friendly and chitchat with them.

A Rock and a Hard Place

There may come a time when a good employee comes to you and says she intends to quit if the bad apple is not let go. While it is important to make it clear that your employees cannot offer you ultimatums or control your management decisions, this is a tough situation. You'll need to weigh the value of the good employee against that of the bad employee. If one is more valuable to your team or company, than that is the person you must choose to stick with. If that means letting a good employee walk, then that is the choice you must make for the good of the company.

MAKE ADVANCEMENT AN OPTION

Another way to retain good employees is to establish a career path for them at your company. It can be very motivating for a good employee to see a way for advancement—both professionally and financially—based on sustained excellence in job performance. During regularly scheduled performance reviews, be sure the path you set for him still meets his goals. The thought of moving up can also make an annoying coworker tolerable because the good apple can see that it is not a permanent situation. Dealing with this kind of workplace headache is much more tolerable when it is understood to be temporary. Also, helping the good apple know that he has control over and can influence the situation through advancement can be a powerful motivational factor to keep him working at your company.

TRAINING

Identifying training that is available to good employees to help them further their careers is a great way to keep them at your company. Employees appreciate the company paying for training because it helps them improve their skills and makes them more marketable in the future. Demonstrating that you have the desire to invest in your team members' success can help them better tolerate some of the potential frustrations caused by bad apples. Training should be both beneficial to the company and the employee and can include daylong seminars for specific tasks or applications or degree-path studies at a local college or university. Some vendors also offer training that can be beneficial to your employees.

REWARD GOOD BEHAVIOR

Praise is one of the most important tools you have at your disposal to influence your employees. Use praise not only to motivate the difficult employees, but also to reward the successes of your good employees, and your team as a whole.

REWARD YOUR BAD APPLES

Rewarding a bad apple is an important way to improve his or her performance, but it's also an important way to help good apples cope. Good employees can tolerate frustrating situations better if they see that the difficult employee is making tangible progress. If tasks or activities are performed better today than yesterday, reinforce that fact to the whole team. For example, pass around a sketch that your difficult employee has created of a new product (as part of his job responsibility) and remark on what a great job it is. At the end of the month or quarter, take a look back with your team and point out how much improvement has been made. This will give your good apples a good feeling about the situation and make them hopeful about the future.

BALANCE CRITICISM WITH PRAISE

All employees require praise and criticism. Your job as a manager is to hand out both, but to try to find a balance that will allow everyone on the team to continue to want to work for you. You should point to and reward the positive steps employees or teams took, even if the overall project was not successful and you have some specific criticisms about the way things were handled. Looking for the silver lining is always worth the effort and finding the right balance between proper praise and corrective criticism can help keep good apples working in the right direction without getting frustrated. Identify the lessons that have been learned from the mistakes made by everyone on the team and that can help turn difficult situations into positive, forward-thinking ones.

MAKE EVERYONE PART OF THE PROCESS

Soliciting input from good employees on how improvements can be made is a great way to help them feel involved and connected to their job and team. This gives them a voice in how to get things done and creates improvement. They can see that you do care and are interested in their input. They feel as though they are a valued part of the team and have some control over the direction the team is going. Employees who feel invested in a team or job are more likely to want to stay.

When getting feedback from employees, it's important not to overstate how you will use their suggestions. Set the right expectations. You don't want them to believe that you will automatically implement everything they suggest without fully considering potential effects, but you also don't want to give lip service and fail to consider ideas that may have some value.

HELPING EMPLOYEES WORK WITH BAD APPLES

While praising and rewarding your employees helps them feel valued, you need to do more to deal with the fact that there is a troublesome employee among them. As a leader, it's essential that you give your employees strategies to use when dealing with a bad apple. You can listen to them complain, but your job will be more difficult if you don't give your good apples tools to help them get through the situation.

Offer Tools

When an employee comes to you with a complaint or problem that is caused or affected by another employee, try to offer real-life solutions that will help that employee work around the problem.

apples to apples A CASE STUDY

Ellen was a paralegal at a large law firm. All the real estate paralegals worked together in a large room. Ellen's desk was next to Kim's and Kim talked to Ellen all the time. Ellen was so distracted by this that she went to her manager, Nancy, to complain. Nancy listened to Ellen's concerns and then offered some concrete suggestions for how to deal with Kim. She suggested that Ellen stop Kim when she is talking and say something like, "I'm sorry, I can't talk right now. I've got to concentrate on this." She also suggested Ellen try to control the chatting—come into work in the morning and talk for a few minutes, then get to work and tell Kim she needed to focus on work. She suggested Ellen institute conversation again later on a break or during lunch. By doing this, Nancy gave Ellen some strategies she could use to take control of the situation. If you can help your employees find strategies that they can use themselves, they will feel more in control of the situation, and you will spend less time mediating conflicts.

Keep It Professional

When you help your employees deal with bad apples, it's important to make sure it doesn't become personal. You want to empower your employees to learn to handle many problems themselves in a professional way, not reinforce their personal complaints about the difficult employee. Every time someone comes into your office to talk, it can't turn into a bitch session about Bad Apple Bob. Instead, redirect the conversation back to the work process or procedure and focus your solution on ways that will move that process forward. If the strategies you are offering your employees are not working, then you need to re-evaluate whether the difficult employee is one you want to keep.

Focus Their Attitudes

Encourage your employees to take a different view when considering situations with difficult coworkers. Suggest that they can look at a situation and ask the following questions:

- What outcome do I want to have?
- How can I control the situation?
- What actions can I take that will have the best chance to achieve the outcome I want?

A good team member taking a confrontational approach with a bad apple will usually not help the situation. Instead, encourage your employees to think of ways they can control their own behavior, which will then have an impact on the problem they're having with the bad apple.

apples to apples A CASE STUDY

Missy is a team leader, Carlos is the team member in charge of generating requisition orders, and Sonya is the team member who faxes requisition orders to the home office. Sonya has a tendency to sit on them because she likes to send them in large batches, which makes her job easier. Carlos has been getting frustrated with this laziness because it makes it look as though he is not getting his work done in a timely manner. Carlos goes to Missy to complain. While Missy is aware of some problems that Sonya causes, she takes the time to talk with Carlos about the way he's approaching Sonya about these problems. She suggests that instead of getting upset and confronting Sonya each time, which she takes as a personal attack, Carlos rephrase his request in a friendly, yet compelling way that Sonya responds to. Negative comments usually generate negative responses. If you can help your employees find positive ways to approach the difficult employee, they're more likely to get positive outcomes.

TECHNOLOGY

Technology can be useful in helping your team deal with a bad apple. It reduces face-to-face contact and provides a record of interactions. E-mail can keep team members apart and reduce the opportunity for conflict. E-mail also allows a manager to be cc'd so he or she knows exactly what's going on and how people are interacting with each other.

Software can be another solution. Project management software allows team members to log in to work on a project and leave notes or progress reports for each other. This kind of communication is more public than e-mail—the whole team can log in and see what's happening, so there is less likely to be intentional sniping.

It's important to note that a reduction of face-to-face interaction can sometimes have the opposite effect—people can lose their connections with each other and not feel personally involved. It's a lot easier to throw stones at someone when you don't know their mother is in the hospital, their dog just died, or that they're nervous about their upcoming real estate licensing exam. Some people are not skilled with words and can send e-mail or leave information in a software program that sends the wrong message, so watch for this as well. If employees are having misunderstandings because of poor wording, step in and offer some training on how to word things.

ACHIEVE BALANCE

When you have a troublesome employee, it's easy to spend a lot of your time assisting, watching, disciplining, working around, or managing him. However, it's a huge mistake to allow this to become your prime objective. You have other employees who need to be managed. Even if they're doing a great job, the fact that there's a bad apple in the bunch is going to influence their work, attitudes, and workflow. Learning how to continue to manage the other employees on your team is of primary importance to both your and your team's success.

You have to find a balance in your management technique. Spend time with those bad apples, but also interact with the rest of your team and offer encouragement, praise, criticism, and input on everything they are doing. It's easy to fall into the "firefighter style of management," and only deal with things when they're on fire and need your attention immediately. However, you can prevent many fires by staying in touch with all employees about all projects.

You've heard the saying, "Idle hands are the devil's workshop." This is true in a team environment. When a team is not busy, people have time to nitpick at each other, find problems, and have the energy to complain. People like to be productive and if you don't provide constructive things for them to do, they'll do something destructive, just to keep busy. This doesn't mean finding busy work for your people, but it does mean keeping them focused on work they can do that will move the team forward.

It is certainly true that an overworked and completely stressed-out team will also react negatively. Your job is to find a good balance so that team members are just busy enough to be happy but not so busy that they're stressed.

Another important aspect of balance is to make sure that you're not only criticizing the difficult employees. Everyone can use some constructive criticism from time to time. A good employee can do things better with a little leadership. Make it clear you are leading and helping your entire team, not just those people who are perceived as bad apples.

KEEP UP GOOD MORALE

Keeping positive morale in your workplace can help counteract the effects of even the worst bad apples. Good employees are better able to tolerate troublesome employees if they are the only truly negative factor in the entire work environment.

Keep your eye out for small things you can do to improve the workplace. They will add up and will help your employees feel valued, while also pushing negativity to the background. For example, if the arm on Sharon's chair is broken, getting that repaired can make her life a lot easier and make it much easier for her to deal with her cubicle mate, Brenda, who is a slob. It could take you a long time to rehabilitate Brenda, but a chair can be fixed in a matter of minutes.

Other small improvements could include:

- Put a coffee machine or small fridge close to the team's work area.
- Turn off officewide music in their section (which some employees find annoying).
- Conduct employee reviews in a timely manner.
- Institute a dress-down day.
- Hold team-building activities—bowling night, summer picnic, etc.
- Schedule team meetings at convenient times so the team is happier to attend them.
- Decorate the environment—plants, natural light, posters, keeping duct work clean, keeping the building clean, emptying garbage, cleaning bathrooms, etc.
- Keep equipment in good working order—getting things fixed or upgrading to equipment that meets their needs will reduce daily frustration levels.

- Sign up for employee discount programs that will benefit your employees.
- Hold a random small drawing or giveaway once a month.
- Buy pizza for a team lunch once a month.

Some managers react negatively to these types of motivators, thinking that the team works for them, but, as a supervisor, your job is to find a way to make your team as productive as possible. A team that is happy and feels cared for will outpace any other team. Working to keep the team happy is not pandering—it's a carefully planned management skill.

GOOD COMMUNICATION CHANNELS

Communication is one of the most important parts of being a manager and maintaining good apples. You need to be able to effectively communicate your thoughts and needs to your employees, and they need to be able to do the same with you. Employees who feel comfortable coming to you with problems, concerns, and suggestions are less likely to become bad apples because you're able to intervene in situations before they create long-term problems.

When You Talk

As a manager, you do a lot of talking with your employees. You're giving them directions, offering feedback, and asking questions. To be effective when you talk to employees, follow these tips:

- Organize your thoughts beforehand when possible, so that you can talk in a clear manner.
- Give information in chunks. Sitting your team down for a one-hour meeting that will have tons of new instructions is

tedious and they're not likely to remember it all. Instead, try to break information up into usable pieces that are easily comprehended and remembered.

- Don't talk too fast. Managers who are nervous or inexperienced tend to talk quickly to cover up their nerves. It's okay to take your time to think things through when you are speaking to an employee or a group of employees.

- Use several kinds of communication. Some people learn by listening, while others are more visual. You need to try to take all of these learning styles into account when you are communicating with your employees. If you need to show an employee a new software program, talk him through it, but also have him walk through it with you. E-mail can be a great way to follow up verbal instructions.

- Don't overcommunicate. If your employees are spending all of their time in meetings or reading memos or e-mail, there isn't a lot of time for work. Find a balance that allows you to communicate important information without overwhelming them.

- Gauge reactions to your communications. Look at the reaction you're getting from your employees. Body language can be an important cue. For example, if employees come to talk to you in your office but don't sit down and instead hover in the doorway, it can be a sign they think if they sit they're going to get roped into a long conversation.

You should also find a balance between friendly chitchat and work talk. It's necessary to have small talk, but it should be a small part of the day and not something that occupies hours of your time. A good manager develops an internal timer for these types of conversations.

Listening Skills

Developing good listening skills takes time and attention. When talking to an employee about work matters, push away all the other things. Focus on the words the employee is saying as well as the nonverbal cues you're getting. Repeat back to the person what he has just told you so that you are certain you understand, and so he is also certain you heard him accurately.

You cannot be a good listener if you're answering e-mail or texts while the person is talking to you. Not only is it visually clear you are not listening, but your attention will be divided and you will not respond appropriately.

DEVELOP TRUST AND RESPECT

Employees who are treated with trust and respect and who feel trust and respect toward their managers are more likely to remain good employees. The simplest rule to keep in mind is this: Say what you mean and do what you say. If you say only things that you mean and intend to follow through on (and do follow through on), your employees will learn they can trust you. As a manager you must be truthful and sometimes you have to say things people don't want to hear. However, if you say them in a respectful way, people will understand (even if they may not like it).

Another aspect of trust and respect has to do with commitment. If you make a commitment to an individual, team, or company, be prepared to take the actions necessary to see it through. Once you show you're committed and follow through, you can ask for and receive that same level of commitment from your employees.

MAKE DECISIONS THAT CONSIDER THE BAD APPLE SITUATION

When assigning work, consider what kind of impact the bad apple is having on other employees. If you know that your shift manager, Dawnlee, has to work closely with Aaron (who is known to be difficult) to accomplish a certain task, be aware of that and don't burden her with a lot of other assignments on top of that one. Be considerate of the stresses that the bad apple places on the team whenever possible.

Again, some managers may balk at this suggestion. After all, your employees are there to do their jobs and the work you assign should be handled, no matter how difficult a coworker is. All we are suggesting is that as a manager you sometimes take a step back and consider the stress that a difficult coworker imposes and what kind of impact that has on your team's ability to do their work. If you are aware of the increase in stress that one employee can create, you can be more sensitive about how you assign work and create expectations. It isn't realistic to think that your employees should just push through and not allow someone who is annoying or difficult to have an impact on their work. Remember, making your good apples feel appreciated and well cared for will create a positive work environment for everyone on the team—and may even convince your bad apples to change their ways.

CHAPTER 7

DEALING WITH PERSONALITY CONFLICTS

Every time you have a workplace with several employees, you have the potential for personality conflicts. It's not reasonable to bring people of different backgrounds, goals, beliefs, experiences, education, and lifestyles together and expect them to get along all of the time. Learning to manage these differences so they don't become a major distraction to your team is an important skill for a manager. Keeping these conflicts under control will help you create a more comfortable workplace, and one where bad apple behavior is minimized.

CH 5. Motivating Bad Apples to Become Good

CH 6. Maintaining Good Apples

CH 7. Dealing with Personality Conflicts

CH 8. Cultivating Conflict Resolution Skills

CH 9. Disciplining Bad Apples

CH 10. Ditching Bad Apples

CH 11. Considering Legal Ramifications

UNDERSTANDING WHY PERSONALITY CONFLICTS ARISE

Some people simply do not work well together. There are a variety of reasons that lead to personality conflicts and it's important to take the time to understand what they may be, so you'll know what to look for.

Some employees have working styles that may be incompatible. If you have one employee who is hyperorganized and always making to-do lists, putting things in alphabetical order, sending coworkers reminders through the office scheduling software program, and keeping tabs on everything, and your other employee is more of a creative type who needs to deal with things in a loose, unscheduled way, it's possible they won't work well together. They do things in totally different ways and may not be able to find a middle ground. However, sometimes coworkers find that their different approaches complement each other. The anal employee can worry about the details on a project while the creative person can look at the big picture and dream up exciting possibilities.

Conflict can also arise based on differing communication styles. Some people are phone people. They would rather talk to you than read an e-mail and respond. Others love e-mail and will use it even when they are sitting next to the person they are contacting. Some employees love meetings; others hate them and don't participate when they have to go. Employees with these differences may find it hard to find a communication strategy they are both comfortable with.

Some people have habits that grate on others—they tap pens, snap gum, drum fingers, say "awesome" all the time, roll their eyes, say hello to everyone who comes near their desk, stack papers insanely neatly, don't put their phone on "do not disturb" when they're away from their desk (so it rings incessantly), pick their nails at their desk, brush crumbs on the floor—the list goes on and on. Lots of people find things like this annoying, but sometimes these habits can make another employee completely nuts.

PREVENTING DIFFERENCES FROM INTERFERING

It sounds simple. You need to keep your employees' personalities from creating conflict. However, if you're the one who needs to find a way for your team to work together, it's far from simple. Differences can and will arise any time you have a group of people who are in contact with each other for extended periods of time. As the manager you should strive to find ways to prevent these conflicts from affecting the workplace and reducing productivity instead of just resigning yourself to conflict.

Avoid Set-in-Stone Conflicts

You need to be sensitive to opposing views. It is probably not a good idea for Michael and Samantha to discuss politics at the office if he is a far-left liberal and she is a tried-and-true conservative. Avoid political references when engaging in idle chitchat or small talk, such as "Did you see what the governor said last night about the cigarette tax?" This only provides an opportunity for Michael and Samantha to express their strong opinions about the situation and get into their differences yet again. A question like "Can you believe the rain we got last week? Can you imagine what would have happened had it been snow?" is a much safer choice. While people may be interested in the weather, they are far less likely to become impassioned when chatting about it.

Clashes occur when you have two people who are different and who allow those differences to get in the way of a smooth working relationship. Personality conflicts can be subterranean—hidden beneath the surface for long periods of time and then brought out by a stressful situation. You may be surprised at what is mentioned when conflict occurs. A minor incident that happened months ago that everyone else has forgotten about can be brought to the surface during a conflict.

If you put any two people together in a room, they can easily find a long list of things they don't agree about or that rub them the wrong way. However, most people are able to work together despite their differences because they have a basic respect for each other. Those who don't have that working respect for their co-workers become unable to get past the basic differences. But the real problem is their lack of respect.

There are several things you can do to prevent minor conflicts from becoming real problems.

1. **Recognize and acknowledge that the conflict exists.** Don't turn your back and assume the people involved are going to work it out on their own.

2. **Take an active approach to the problem that is developing.** Watch for potential problems and step in to cool them down before they become big conflicts that interfere with work.

3. **Take a zero-tolerance approach.** Make it clear to your team that you aren't going to allow petty resentments, arguments, and tiffs to derail your team.

4. **Work with your team to help everyone develop respect for each other.** Emphasize how important respect is and make it a basic goal for your team. Team building activities are a great way for people to come to know and understand each other. Respect develops out of personal connections like these.

WHEN YOU ARE A PARTY TO THE CONFLICT

There are times when you find that you have a personality conflict with an employee you're managing. If you're working with someone who pushes all your buttons and makes you want to scream, it can be challenging to think clearly about the situation and take action that is not clouded by emotions.

Always think before reacting when you're dealing with someone who upsets or annoys you. If an immediate response is needed, take a breath and start by restating the situation ("You're saying that you've been significantly late six out of the last nine workdays because you've hit heavy traffic.") This will give you time to consider an appropriate response. If you can sit on it overnight, do so. It's okay to write the e-mail or prepare the response, but wait until the next day or after lunch to send it out. You may find that when you reread it, it doesn't have the message you intended.

It's important to separate behavior that annoys you from behavior that has a negative impact on the company. There are times when annoying behavior becomes so irritating that it interferes with your ability to work or to function, even though it may not have a direct impact on productivity. Other times though, if something is just annoying but doesn't have any other impact, brush it off and don't get involved. You don't need to have a showdown over every comment one of your employees makes to you.

Consider how your own actions are contributing to the situation. This can be difficult to admit to yourself, but a good manager should be able to objectively evaluate her own performance. You may be asking questions or giving directions in a way that is causing the employee's grating response. Think about what you can do to remove these opportunities for difficult behavior.

When you are having a conflict with an employee, keep in mind that your role is to be the bigger person in the conflict. Always strive to be the voice of reason, the adult who won't get into it. Your goal should be to never escalate conflict. That's easy to say, but when you're in the heat of the moment dealing with an employee who drives you nuts, it can be hard to remember. Always keep in mind that you are the one setting the tone, creating the expectations, and providing the model for behavior. If you shout at an employee, you've given him license to shout back at you. When you're involved in conflict with an employee, remember that you're the manager and the ultimate power rests with you. A good manager doesn't need to exercise that power often, but should always be aware that she holds it. This will give you an air of authority that will end the majority of conflicts with employees before they can get out of hand.

CONFLICT BETWEEN TWO TEAM MEMBERS

If you have two people on your team who are like oil and water, it can be hard to find a way to get them to put their differences aside and work together for the benefit of the team. It's important that you find a way to do so, however, because their conflict is distracting not only to them, but also to the rest of your team.

Just Grow Up!
You may get tired of having to deal with squabbles among team members. Some of them can seem very silly and petty. It's tempting to just shout "Grow up!" and, honestly, this can be an effective tactic. It shocks the two people into realizing how immature and ridiculous they are being. However, you should be careful not to dismiss real complaints or ignore big problems.

INTERVENING

If you have two people in your office who are having a problem with each other, it's your responsibility as their manager to put an end to the problem, or at least find a way to get it under control. The first thing you should do is stop any escalation. You have to get the two people who are going at it to stop talking and break eye contact. The easiest way to do this is to physically separate them. Tell them to go back to their desks, or send one off to run an errand. Get them away from each other so you can ease the immediate tension and keep things from getting worse. They need breathing room so they can both calm down. If you don't know what to say in a situation like this, approach the two people and say, "That's enough," "Stop right now," or "I want you both to go back to your desks and take a breath."

> **Waterworks**
>
> If one or both people involved are women, you may have a situation that involves tears. Some male managers are flabbergasted by crying in the workplace and don't know how to handle it. If you encounter this, you first have to end the immediate conflict and get the two people involved away from each other. Next, give the one who is crying some privacy; suggest she go to the bathroom or take a walk. If the person crying is very upset, it is a good idea to assign a neutral female team member to go with her to make sure she is okay.

If you aren't sure how to get them to physically separate, consider which employee is the more reasonable one. Usually there is one that you know you can easily manage. Use your influence on him and send him out of the room. Obviously, if you ever have a conflict that escalates into something physical you need to call for help. Don't try to get in the middle of it.

Once you have stopped the verbal escalation, you have time to consider how to deal with the problem. Talk to each person individually to find out what happened, or what set them off. You can then take appropriate disciplinary steps if necessary.

You want to be sure that the conflict does not start up again once you leave the room, and there's a good chance it could. Even a simple look can set these things off. If the situation is really bad, you may have to decide to send one or both people home for the day to get some space.

DEALING WITH PERSONALITY PROBLEMS

While you may sometimes have big blowups between employees, it's more common to have small conflicts in which people pick away at each other or have undercurrents of bad feelings. Most of the time, it's best to just stay out of these situations and let them resolve themselves, but if the situation becomes too distracting and interferes with productivity, you've got to step in.

apples to apples A CASE STUDY

Laurie was irritated by her coworker Joel's constant humming and spoke to her manager, Carol, about the situation. Carol thought about the scenario and decided to talk to Joel about what was going on. She pulled Joel aside and said, "I know you probably don't realize you're doing this, but you hum all the time and it has become a distraction. I need you to stop." She didn't tell Joel that he was driving Laurie crazy and she had spoken to Carol about it. Carol made the conversation about Joel's behavior, not Laurie's complaint.

Sometimes you'll have two people who get on each other's nerves for no reason you can really see or understand. You can talk to each one and try to minimize the behavior and traits that are aggravating the other person, but putting some physical space between them is often the best plan.

Understand and accept that you can't eliminate these kinds of mild conflict completely. Your office is not the Good Ship Lollipop and there will always be stress and conflict going on. In fact, sometimes you can use the situation to your advantage. An undercurrent of resentment or dislike among team members can act as a system of checks and balances at times. If both parties report back to you on what the other is doing wrong, you'll have some inside information about your team that can be very valuable. This isn't the same as tattling. You want to have a rapport with your employees that allows them to tell you what's troubling them or making their jobs harder. This is merely another part of having open communication. You shouldn't encourage people to backstab each other, but you need to have a relationship with your employees that allows them to feel comfortable talking with you about problems within the team.

GENDER

When looking at a conflict, consider the gender of the people involved. It's more common for women to have ongoing conflicts with other women than with men, or men with other men. When men have personality conflicts with other men, they tend to resolve them quickly. Men often will have an immediate confrontation and either resolve it or come to a conclusion that the situation is what it is and then simply move on and ignore it. Women tend to remember specific issues and bring them up in conflicts again and again. Men will generally know there's a problem, but will let go of the specifics over time.

When two women have a problem with each other, it docs not frequently result in a screaming match or other overt conflict. Instead, you're more likely to find that they use some of the sneakier bad apple behaviors discussed in Chapter 2. Backstabbing is a very common practice. Women also talk about each other behind each other's backs and may use cold shoulders to leave people out. They also can form cliques within the team.

These kinds of situations are hard to identify and even harder to intervene in as a manager. If it is clear to you that this kind of behavior is happening and that productivity is being impaired, you need to step in and do something, even if the situation feels childish. Make a stand and tell the person or people perpetrating the bad behavior that it has to stop. Part of that employee's job is to be civil to the other people on the team. If you get an employee who answers you by saying, "But I don't like her, why should I have to be nice to her?" your answer must be that it is part of her job to do so, and if she can't, then you'll have to choose between the two employees involved.

Signs You Cannot Let a Conflict Ride
If you see these types of behavior, you'll know you need to step in and take action:

- Aggressive behavior
- Physical contact
- Shouting
- Disruption to others
- Tears
- A conflict that is frequently repeated

It can be very hard at times for female managers to stand up and talk decisively to a team member in this way. If a man does this, he's seen as a tough boss, but if a woman does it, she's a b*tch or it's "that time of the month." If you are a woman and a manager, you have to have the guts to discipline and direct your employees when they are off track, no matter the situation. It's your responsibility to keep your team in line and if that means people criticize your unfeminine behavior, then that is their problem.

HELP THE INNOCENT PARTY

If the conflict involves a person who, for the most part, is innocent and not an instigator, you should work with him to help him learn how to deal with these kinds of conflicts. For example, if Ty is the office bully and meek Dave is his frequent target, you should talk with Dave and help him learn how to end the conflict on his own (of course talking to Ty is also your responsibility). There will be times when you aren't around to rescue Dave, so you need to empower him to find solutions without you. Then, the two people involved will either resolve the conflict themselves, or it will end up coming back to you for resolution. If they can come to a resolution on their own, then they have reached a level of working respect that will prevent future conflicts from happening.

CONFLICT BETWEEN ONE PERSON AND MANY OTHERS

If you have one person on your team who has trouble getting along with many members of your team, you may conclude that she's a bad apple and decide to get rid of her. While she might have some annoying characteristics or behavior that turn people off, the real problem may be that your team is not open-minded.

It's possible to have a team that together has an overall personality problem—it's called attitude!

One possible scenario: one bad apple on your team is rallying the rest of the team against one employee. A one-to-one conflict can elevate to a team-versus-one-person conflict in this way. You need to try to deconstruct what's happening and, when you do, you'll discover the problem is really between two people. You can then deal with that problem and the team problem will go away.

Sometimes the team will mutually decide they don't like or don't respect someone on the team. Every time MaryAnn is out, it's "pick on MaryAnn day." The team will make jokes about her and bond over how much they don't like her. It's your role to step in and stop this behavior. MaryAnn isn't there to hear it, but this creates a hostile work environment. When she returns, she can probably sense the feelings that have been aired against her. If you allow it, you're giving your team license to do this to others.

No matter what, you absolutely cannot join in on this kind of joking. Even if the situation hasn't evolved into a hostile one in which the whole team hates MaryAnn, you can't say anything negative about her, even in a joking way, because then you are condoning the bad apple behavior. Humor can be very useful as a management tool, but the only safe person to make fun of is you. It's too easy to cross the line and actually hurt an employee's feelings when poking fun.

OVERACHIEVERS VS. YOUR TEAM

Many times an overachiever can be a source of conflict among a team of status quo'ers. An employee who wants to advance may not be doing so in an appropriate way. Be sure to examine the dynamics before responding to a team indication that one person is not working out. You can't base your opinion of a team member solely on what others think. Violet may be a career climber who is stepping on people's toes left and right, but she may also be your best producer. Her value to the team outweighs the general unhappiness she is causing. You can try to talk to her about being more sensitive to others, but you certainly don't want to fire her just because people grumble about her. You can, however, talk to the team as a whole and explain to them that you expect them to treat her with respect at all times.

CONFLICTS AMONG TEAMS

When two teams have a conflict with each other, it can make things uncomfortable for everyone in the company and can create a situation that makes it hard for the company to meet goals. If your team is involved in this kind of situation, defuse it immediately.

MANAGEMENT CONFLICT

If your team is experiencing conflict with another team, the problem can often be traced to a problem between you and the other manager. You may have a personality conflict, or you might have differing professional goals that are causing clashes. You're both responsible for how your teams behave and, if they're not getting along, the ultimate responsibility comes back to the two of you. Even if you don't talk to your team about the problem (and you certainly shouldn't if you can avoid it!), they can often sense it. Strive to resolve your problems with the other manager so that they do not affect your team. Sit down with the other manager and come up with a solution that allows you to have a working relationship. If there's a problem, find possible answers. If the other manager is a complete jerk, there may be no solution other than to minimize conflict and try to work around the barriers he's put up to your team's success.

SOLUTIONS

Remember that managers always set the tone. Model how you want your team to behave around the other team. Talk to them about the importance of the other team and encourage them to work with a spirit of cooperation.

Cross-team building activities can be very helpful. It's common for people to have misconceptions about those they don't know or understand. Develop an education program within your company that helps workers become familiar with other jobs and responsibilities within the company. Sponsor a luncheon for the two teams together so they can spend some time with each other and develop personal connections.

Signs a Conflict Is Brewing

Look for these signs that indicate when a conflict is about to happen:

- Glaring
- Unfriendly nonverbal communication (such as slamming things)
- A hostile tone in e-mail
- Unfriendly body language (crossed arms, inability to look at someone)
- A curt or unfriendly tone of speech
- Huddled talking among employees
- Tension in the air

Set goals that the teams can work to meet together. Common goals are a powerful motivating factor. If the teams have to create cooperation to achieve goals, they will find they can work together and rely on each other.

Sometimes you may think you have a team-versus-team problem, when in reality you have two people on different teams who are at odds and manage to draw their entire team into the conflict with them. Ask questions and get to the root of the problem and then resolve it as a one-to-one dispute. Advise your team to stay out of the conflict.

PHYSICAL RESTRUCTURING

One of the easiest ways to put a stop to a problem between employees is to separate them. In essence, you're sending them to their separate preschool timeout corners. A little distance can work a lot of magic. Rearrange the seating in your area. Make sure they sit at opposite ends of the conference table. Don't send them out of town together. Put them on different projects.

You can't be a playground monitor and always be looking over their shoulders, so you have to expect them to respect the distance you create. If they have no reason to talk to each other, they shouldn't have to come in contact. In a small office there's no way to completely avoid another person, but it is possible to minimize the contact that happens.

When you use physical restructuring to minimize conflict, keep in mind that the move should not appear to anyone to be a reward or a punishment. For example, if Tamara and Jeannette don't get along and you decide to split them up, don't move Jeannette to the back of the office next to the loud air-conditioning unit, because it will appear to be a reprimand. Similarly, don't move Tamara up front next to the window, because that could come off looking like a reward. Additionally, don't move one of them to a nicer desk, a crummier computer, or next to her best buddy.

Tips for Minimizing Conflicts in a Small Office
Some ways to reduce problems in a physically small office space include:

- Create automated workflows to minimize interaction requirements.
- Keep them busy—employees with a steady flow of work have less time to get into spats with each other.
- Find projects that allow each person to shine while working together. This can help bring them together.
- If you don't have room to put physical space between two people's work areas, at least arrange things so that they sit back to back. Out of sight, out of mind!
- Reward good performance when they get along.
- Don't tolerate bad behavior. In a smaller office, you don't have the time or energy to deal with this, so don't put up with it. Simply tell them to stop and if they don't, write them up or provide other consequences.

JOB RESPONSIBILITY REALLOCATION

Another option to defuse a conflict is to change job responsibilities so that the people in the conflict don't have to work together a lot. A change in job responsibility should not be confused with a change in jobs. We're not talking about promoting or demoting people here; instead we're talking about changing what their job description is. If Celeste and Darren can never agree about brochure designs, changing Darren's responsibilities so that he no longer works on brochure designs and instead handles business card designs is a change that has put some figurative space between the two of them. They no longer will be working on the same projects, so their conflict will be minimized.

If you consider changing job responsibilities in order to manage a personality conflict, make sure that the employees are still being used to their greatest potential. Whatever change you implement must be good for the company. It is not helpful to give someone responsibilities he can't handle or is not skilled at—the long-term effect will be a loss of productivity.

If you change job responsibilities to reduce a conflict, make sure you consider the personalities the person will come into contact with under the new responsibilities. You don't want to create a situation that is worse than the one you're dealing with in the first place. Consider the skills your employee has and try to maximize those skills with the new responsibilities.

When you change one person's job responsibilities, be careful to ensure that it doesn't look like a promotion or demotion. If one person is moved to a new, exciting account, the other person in the conflict might feel penalized or resentful, which can breed more bad apple behavior.

ORGANIZATIONAL RESTRUCTURING

Organizational restructuring involves altering who reports to whom and how the chain of responsibility falls through your team. This isn't a job change or a change in job responsibility, but instead a shift within the chain of command. If Tricia sends her monthly spreadsheets to Paul (whom she hates), who then crunches her numbers along with some others before passing it along to the VP of that department, you could reorganize things so that Tricia's spreadsheets go directly to the VP, or change things around so Paul and Tricia send their numbers to someone else who then crunches them and sends them to the VP.

Reorganization is a good solution when you have two people who can't work well together, but you must always be sure that the change will serve the company's needs. You do not want to create more work or another layer of bureaucracy just to keep two people from bickering.

SENSITIVITY TRAINING

Sensitivity training is workplace training that helps people become aware of their own prejudices.

But be careful with it. If you single out one person for sensitivity training, you're calling attention to him and essentially punishing him for his views. The best way to use sensitivity training is to have your entire team undergo the training without singling anyone out. Clearly, sensitivity training is not a catchall solution, but many companies make it mandatory because it places them in a better position should they face a discrimination case.

The biggest mistake managers make with regard to sensitivity or diversity training is assuming that, by arranging the training session, they have solved the problem. The session merely offers workers tools for handling the conflicts they face—it in no way solves them. Your role is to help your employees follow through on what they've learned and put it into action.

Sometimes understanding the different personalities of your team members and working to resolve those differences on your own isn't enough. If you and your team can't work together to solve the problems that are keeping you from reaching your goals, you may have to resort to conflict resolution to try to solve the problem.

CHAPTER 8

CULTIVATING CONFLICT RESOLUTION SKILLS

If trouble is brewing in your office or there is ongoing conflict involving a bad apple, you need to have some solid skills that will help you defuse or resolve the long-term problems that are happening between your employees. Conflict resolution, a set procedure in which workplace conflict is resolved through mediation, sounds like a big fancy process, but in an office setting it's just a way of trying to smooth out the problems between two employees in a civilized, face-to-face way.

CH 5. Motivating Bad Apples to Become Good

CH 6. Maintaining Good Apples

CH 7. Dealing with Personality Conflicts

CH 8. Cultivating Conflict Resolution Skills

CH 9. Disciplining Bad Apples

CH 10. Ditching Bad Apples

CH 11. Considering Legal Ramifications

Every manager has conflict resolution skills, and learning to enhance yours will help you create a more successful team. Conflict resolution is an important process, but because it's often a formal process within a company, it can take things to the next level in terms of HR response or involvement.

WHY YOU NEED CONFLICT RESOLUTION

When two employees have a long-lasting problem with each other, often this causes an undercurrent of conflict. They aren't screaming in each other's faces, but the conflict between them flares up at times and remains just below the surface the rest of the time. A lot of times this happens when you have two people who just aren't able to work together smoothly. Allowing this kind of undercurrent to continue is unhealthy not only for the people involved, but also for the team. It's not good for anyone to work in an atmosphere in which hostility and occasional blowups are common. It is a distraction and it has an impact on productivity. People may be walking around on tiptoes, waiting for the blowups to happen.

When you choose conflict resolution, you do so because the issue involved has become such a distraction or a problem that your next step is terminating one of the employees. You've tried talking to each person, offering suggestions, and adjusting things to accommodate their issue, but it hasn't worked. If they are not worth the time and effort involved in a conflict resolution process, you need to move toward termination.

It's important to not use conflict resolution as a way to escape the fact that you need to terminate someone. If you really know that a person is not working out or has insurmountable personality issues, no amount of conflict resolution is going to turn things around. You're wasting not only your time, but that of the other employee involved. You're not giving your bad apple an extra chance or being accommodating—you're wasting resources, which is not good for your team or company. When someone clearly needs to be fired, it's best to just do it quickly and get it over with so your team can move on. You'll learn more about how to fire a bad apple in Chapter 10.

Conflict resolution is not generally useful when you already know who is right and who is wrong in the situation. In that instance, you as the manager need to tell the employees what to do and how to handle things. Conflict resolution is for when it is not clear to you who is right or wrong—all you can see is that the two people can't agree or work together and that this is creating a problem for your team. If Dana and Christy are having a problem about who should process orders for the new ID cards and it's clearly stated as part of Christy's job description, conflict resolution is useless. Instead, point out that it is Christy's responsibility.

When you have a bad apple that you really can't fire, conflict resolution can be helpful. You know this person is probably the one in the situation who is wrong, but, since you can't fire him, you need to work things out so that the two employees can coexist and work together. You may not be able to solve the underlying problem, but you may be able to help the two people involved find a way to work together that is less stressful.

Note that this process is most effective when you are dealing with defined issues on a specific project or procedure and not when you are dealing with long-term personality issues. The goal of the meeting is not only to come to a solution for the problem at hand, but also to help the two people reach a place where they can avoid future problems.

HOW TO BRING PARTIES TOGETHER

When two people have an underlying conflict, you can try the many solutions recommended in the last chapter, such as keeping them away from each other, providing incentives for both of them, and changing workflow so they don't influence each other's work. These can be very workable solutions, but sometimes circumstances won't allow you to keep them apart, incentives don't work, or their work is integral to each other. When this happens, you need a solution. The conflict resolution process brings them together in a neutral setting to try to resolve the problem between them.

Interteam Conflict Resolution

When you need conflict resolution between a member of your team and a member of another team, you and the other manager need to spend some time talking about the situation. Resort to conflict resolution only when other solutions have not worked. It's easy for this situation to turn into a two-against-two scenario, so you and the other manager need to work together and focus on finding a solution that works for everyone in the room. For example, Sharon from accounting and Ray from shipping work together to ensure that customers are notified of proper charges by invoice. Both employees are good at what they do, but there's a strong personality clash between them. Each person's manager spoke separately with his or her own employee, but the situation continued to fester and now has an impact on the quality of their work. If a solution is not found, one or both employees may have to be replaced. To avoid this, a face-to-face meeting to resolve the differences with the employees and managers is required.

If you reach the point where conflict resolution is necessary, it's a good idea to talk with your HR department to find out if the company has guidelines for this situation. In some large companies, HR will facilitate the process. Some very large companies have conflict resolution specialists on staff.

Once you've determined that you need to set up a conflict resolution meeting, notify the two employees together. It's going to be really important that you remain as neutral as possible throughout this process, so if you talk to Sharon personally in the break room, but send Ray an e-mail, you've already set things up unequally. Talk to them together if possible. If not, send them the same e-mail or say the same thing to each of them in the same place.

When you explain that you're setting up a meeting to work through the issue or issues, keep it simple without finger pointing. You don't want to say, "I want to set up a meeting so we can figure out why you are getting so angry with Sharon." Instead, say, "I'm setting up a meeting so that we can resolve the issues or concerns that each of you has expressed."

Neutrality in Question

If one of the employees thinks you're not handling the situation in a neutral manner (or if you have an underlying conflict with that person), it can be helpful to bring in a third party to assist with the meeting (such as your boss or another manager). The downside of this is that it sends a clear message to your entire team that you are, in fact, not neutral at all.

You want to set a positive tone, so don't threaten, "If you can't work this out in this meeting, one of you will be fired." If anything, that kind of statement will make things worse and will set things up to be more aggressively adversarial. The employees will each spend the meeting trying to show that the other person should be fired instead of trying to resolve the issue.

When you arrange the meeting, be clear that you are setting up a conflict resolution meeting. Tell your employees that they are both valuable employees and you want to find a way to work things out so that they can work together more smoothly. It can be useful to mention that they should come to the meeting in the spirit of cooperation because the goal is to work out a solution that both of them can live with. Help them get into the right frame of mind before the meeting even begins.

FORMAT FOR MEETINGS

When you have a conflict resolution meeting, keep in mind that you want to create a comfortable setting and meeting format that will allow them to relax and feel empowered.

Hold the meeting in a neutral setting. Your team's conference room might be a good place, but if you know the entire team can hear every word that is said through the walls, it may not be ideal. You want to give at least some perception of privacy. Your office may be a neutral place, but if one of the team members is your assistant who spends a lot of time in your office, this may appear to give her an advantage. A conference room or office in another part of the building may be a good solution.

Schedule the meeting at a time when no one is being crushed by a deadline and not at the end of the day when everyone just wants to go home. It may be a good idea to have the meeting outside of normal business hours. If your office starts at 9 A.M., suggest an 8 A.M. meeting. This way workflow isn't disrupted and your employees won't feel that everyone in the office is watching.

Make the purpose of the meeting clear at the beginning. Reiterate to them that you're not there to blame anyone for the problem. You are, however, the boss and it is up to you to choose a solution if necessary. You're not going to sit by and let your two employees make a decision you don't agree with—or not come to any decision at all. Generally though, if they can agree on something, they're much more likely to follow through on it than if you choose a solution for them to follow. If they can't agree, you'll choose the solution and they'll have to live with it. You really want to encourage them to work this out themselves, though. A solution that they both agree on is much more likely to succeed than one you impose on them.

Lay ground rules for the meeting, which can include:

- A time limit expectation—a general idea of how long you will meet for (and the understanding that it may take more than one meeting)
- A clear agenda of what is on the table for discussion or what the issue is that needs to be resolved and what you're hoping to accomplish from the meeting
- No raised voices, insults, or curse words
- Turn-taking and not talking over the other person

Make the kind of solution you're aiming for clear. Your goal isn't to resolve every difference they have. Instead, it can be helpful to focus on the issues they're having with a certain project or circumstance. Deal only with that project in your meeting. You may need to meet again for the next project, but eventually they'll learn to apply the techniques you've shown them to resolve future problems.

AVOIDING ESCALATION

Sometimes, when you bring two people together in an attempt to talk through or find solutions to problems, you can end up making things worse. If you bring two team members together, it's up to you to make sure you control the tone and progress of the meeting.

Set clear expectations about the meeting beforehand so no one is blindsided. This can help reduce tension in the meeting and allow the employees to talk more freely.

In Over Your Head

There are some conflicts that can't be resolved, and some of them can be traced back to the basic bad apple personality traits we identified in Chapter 2. You're not a therapist and you're not going to be able to get to the root of why someone acts in a passive-aggressive way. You can't solve basic personality problems. Sometimes, you simply need to recognize that the conflict between your two employees is far beyond your conflict resolution skills. If you keep banging away at it, you're probably going to make things worse. In these situations you need to either find a way to work around the conflict, or think about firing the employee who is causing the problems.

Escalation commonly occurs when people feel backed into a corner or ganged up on and have to defend themselves. Of course, defensiveness is a common reaction in this kind of meeting, but you want to minimize this reaction since it does not help you get to real solutions. If you're meeting with Koko and Hannah and both you and Koko focus on Hannah's disorganization and hammer away at her about how she just has to pull it together, you're not running a conflict resolution meeting, you're chastising Hannah. If you have issues with Hannah's performance, discuss them with her in private. The purpose of the meeting should be to create a plan that will allow Hannah and Koko to work together without hostility. The disorganization may be one factor, but there are other components.

"I" Statements

Encourage the two participants to try to talk in "I" statements. Instead of starting everything off in an accusatory way—"you always do this" or "you make me crazy when you . . ." —suggest they speak in statements that begin with "I." "I would be better able to handle the orders if we did it this way" or "I feel really uncomfortable when you proofread my press releases."

Body language is often the first sign that a conversation is moving past a civil tone. It's natural for people to be tense in such a meeting, but very agitated movements can be warning signs.

You should also watch for body language that shows the person has withdrawn from the conversation. These include:

- Eye rolling
- Looking elsewhere
- Nail picking
- Crossed arms

If things seem to be getting heated, point the conversation in a positive direction. Take inflammatory statements made by the people in the meeting and restate them in a more civil way to keep the conversation on task. For example, if Gwen says to Katie, "You're always late and it makes me crazy. It screws up the whole day because you can't get your butt out of bed!" You can restate this by saying, "Gwen is saying that because you aren't here on time some days, it's difficult for the team to get things started." You've reframed the conversation to focus on the issue, not on the emotions.

People also offer verbal cues when they have withdrawn. If one of the participants says "Yeah, whatever" or "Mmm hmmm," she's checking out of the conversation. When this happens, you need to draw the person back into the conversation by asking questions or directing suggestions to that person. Sometimes you won't be able to bring a person back in if she's decided to check out and be done—you can't force someone to be constructive, but you can point out to them how important it is to come to a resolution.

Taking a break can be a great way to clear the air for a little bit and let everyone gather their thoughts. You shouldn't keep your two employees locked in a room and tell them they can't leave until they come to a resolution. Sometimes you have to tell them you're stopping for now and want everyone to get back to work and come back tomorrow ready to try again.

DETERMINING THE ROOT OF THE CONFLICT

Sometimes it can be challenging to find out what the real problem is in the conflict. When there's been lingering tension between two people for a while, the initial conflict may have gotten lost. As a manager, you need to figure out what the ongoing problem is between the employees so you can work toward a resolution.

It can be helpful to ask each person to describe the root of the conflict. This can be very revealing and help you understand that person's point of view. It can also be helpful for you to present what the conflict looks like from your perspective—when you see it flaring and what situations, processes, jobs, clients, and so on seem to bring it up. You may be able to identify a pattern that they cannot.

If you determine that this problem cannot be solved through this intervention, and that, instead, these are just two people (one probably a bad apple) who have personalities that do not mesh and never will, you've actually found the root of the conflict and can proceed to a solution (find a way to work around the personality problems, or fire one of them) using that as your basis.

FINDING COMMON GROUND

One of the easiest ways to bring people together is to help them realize that they have some things in common, which could include:

- Similar lifestyle (they are both mothers, grad students, country dwellers, etc.)
- A shared desire to see the team or company succeed
- Common interests (sports, music, TV shows, hobbies, etc.)

The most important commonality is the desire to find a solution to their conflict in the meeting. They are also (presumably) both committed to their jobs and want to succeed at them (or at least want to continue receiving their paychecks!). Tying the outcome of the meeting to job success is an important way to help them see the benefit of conflict resolution.

When you are helping them talk through the problem, it can be useful to point out the areas they agree about. "Okay, so you both think that the dictation should be stored in this file." Even if the things they agree upon are minimal, highlight them. Once you get two people into the mindset of agreement, they will most likely want to continue agreeing. Emphasizing agreement tends to deemphasize disagreement and they may find they agree on more things than they disagree on, making it easier for them to work together.

MANAGING YOURSELF IN CONFLICT RESOLUTION

It can be easy to lose sight of the fact that, in addition to managing the two employees in the meeting, you also need to manage yourself. If the meeting is not going well, it's easy to get frustrated and let the frustration show. There are certainly times when exhibiting frustration can be helpful and will move people along, but it should be used in a calculated way and not simply because you cannot control it.

Make sure you really listen to what your employees are saying. Too many managers come to conflict resolution meetings with preconceived notions about what the problem is or what kind of solution should be created. Instead, remain open to everything and pay attention to what your employees are saying. It's possible there are things going on you had no idea about.

Be prepared to accept failure. If the employees cannot work together, there isn't going to be any solution that will fix that. You can't make it work through sheer power of your will.

IDENTIFYING RESOLUTION PATHWAYS

Once you've reached a point where you really understand the cause of the conflict, you can then work toward a solution. Although you're trying to get your two employees to have a meeting of the minds, you're the one who will identify and implement the solution. You want their input and agreement, but you're the one who will make the ultimate decision about what the plan is going to be.

A solution is a path that will alleviate or eliminate the conflict between the employees. You have to remember that you can't easily change the way people feel, but you can change how they react to things. Remember, the more specific the solution, the better chance for success. A solution should set out some actions that your employees will take, or things they will *not* do. Offer tangible, measurable results so you'll be able to track their progress (or lack thereof).

Once you have a plan, you should schedule an immediate follow-up. Depending on the situation, you could agree to meet again in two weeks to monitor how the plan has worked. This is important so that each employee feels he has a way to respond if there is a continued problem.

IMPLEMENTATION

Determining how you're going to solve the conflict is one thing, but actually putting the solution into place is another. It's easy to feel at the close of the meeting that you can close the book on the problem. In most cases, you can't. You have to take whatever solution you've found and actually implement it in the workplace.

First, document what was decided on in the meeting so everyone can refer to the written plan. Make sure that the way you write up the plan is even-handed, so both sides feel that they're respected and have an equal part. Ask each person to commit to the written plan, either by signing a piece of paper or responding affirmatively to an e-mail containing it. Keep a copy of this agreement in both of their files.

FOLLOW THROUGH

Implementing the solution is only the first step in a long-term plan. You need to follow up and make sure the solution is working. You may find you need to tweak the plan occasionally to keep it in good working order. You'll also have to watch for compliance—you can't assume that just because they tell you they're working the plan that they actually are. Check up on them and find out if they are in fact doing what they are supposed to do.

It's critical that you follow through on your end and demonstrate your commitment to making the solution work. Be sure to follow up closely in the weeks following the meeting. Your intent should be to gradually let go of the situation and let the new plan become a part of the normal course of work. Eventually, it should just be part of the way business is done.

IMPACT ON THE TEAM

When a situation with two employees results in a conflict resolution meeting, it will have an impact on your team. You don't want this conflict or its resolution to become a distraction, so your team shouldn't be involved. You do, however, want the team to be supportive of the solution and its implementation. Minimize the tangible impact on the team and be sure that the improvements make the workplace run more smoothly for everyone.

CONFLICT RESOLUTION FAILURE

If the employees cannot reach an agreement and you can't find a solution, then the conflict resolution attempt has failed. This is when you need to decide what action you are going to take—

most likely terminating an employee if you have already exhausted all other options.

Another situation is one in which a solution is found and agreed upon, but one or both people do not follow through with it. In this situation, find out what happened. It could be that the solution needs to be tweaked a bit to work. The solution may also end up being entirely unworkable. Here, again, you're faced with a choice about termination.

apples to apples A CASE STUDY

Chandra is the manager of a new product development team, Annie works in research, and Tomas is in product development. Annie runs the focus groups and then gives the results to Tomas, who needs to take the results into consideration when he creates prototypes. Tomas has a big ego and insists that Annie doesn't ask the right questions in her focus groups, so he dismisses the information she brings him. They get into heated discussions about this at product meetings. Chandra cannot separate them—their roles are integral to development. She has tried telling Tomas to be more respectful of Annie in meetings and suggested that Annie put some more thought into her focus group questions. None of this has helped. The conflict between them is making it difficult for the entire team, and Chandra worries how it's affecting their products.

Chandra sets up a conflict resolution meeting with Annie and Tomas. They spend a long time talking over the situation and, in the course of the conversation, it becomes clear that Tomas has always thought he should be able to suggest some questions to Annie before she holds focus group meetings, but has never communicated this. Annie is not opposed, thinks it will probably stop him from being so full of himself at product meetings, and agrees. Tomas agrees that he will not undermine her in the meetings and is happy to be able to pose suggestions.

Things go seemingly well on the next project until they get to the product meeting after the focus groups. Tomas feels Annie listens to him but doesn't implement anything he suggests. Annie feels that Tomas doesn't offer workable questions and doesn't understand the dynamics of a focus group.

Chandra decides to talk with them together and to go over the details of what happened on the last project and how to proceed in the future. By sitting down and talking over a specific project, Annie is able to explain to Tomas the types of questions she can ask in a focus group, and Tomas can point out areas where the focus group information doesn't give him the details he needs. They finally understand each other and Tomas is able to offer specific details to Annie and she is able to format those questions so they work in her focus group.

CHAPTER 9

DISCIPLINING BAD APPLES

When working with challenging employees, using discipline effectively and appropriately is a key factor in determining how successful you will be as a manager. Every manager must be prepared to use discipline to enforce rules, standards, and expectations. In a perfect world, a good manager wouldn't have to use discipline, because he would motivate people to do everything properly. In the real world, no manager is perfect and not every group of employees can be motivated to work without problems all the time.

CH 5. Motivating Bad Apples to Become Good

CH 6. Maintaining Good Apples

CH 7. Dealing with Personality Conflicts

CH 8. Cultivating Conflict Resolution Skills

CH 9. Disciplining Bad Apples

CH 10. Ditching Bad Apples

CH 11. Considering Legal Ramifications

WHAT IS DISCIPLINE?

There is a difference between discipline and criticism. Criticism is when you point out what is wrong and offer advice as to what should be done instead. Discipline is used when you need to stop a behavior or reprimand an employee for behavior that is inappropriate or detrimental to the team or company.

Criticism: I'd like you to use blue ink when filling out this form. You need to stop using red ink.

Discipline: The next time you use red ink on this form, I'm going to write you up.

Discipline can consist of a variety of things in the workplace:

- Verbal warning
- Written warning
- Docking pay
- Reducing pay rate
- Reducing hours
- Demotion
- Removing responsibilities
- Removing privileges or perks.

Criticism is an inherent part of instruction and training. Discipline comes into play when an employee who should know better makes a mistake. It is always best to start with the lowest form of discipline when dealing with a problem and move up the ladder. Severe incidents, of course, warrant more heavy-handed discipline.

CONSTRUCTIVE CRITICISM

Offering criticism in a constructive way is often a very effective way to change an employee's performance or behavior. Constructive criticism points out to the employee what he has done wrong and why it is wrong, and also shows him how to improve.

The most important thing to remember about constructive criticism is that it truly must be constructive. Too often managers use constructive criticism as an excuse to say negative things. They will say, "If I can offer some constructive criticism here," and then go on to provide a laundry list of things that are wrong. The whole point is that you must offer some positive, helpful thoughts or direction. You're not there to tell the employee how great she is, but you should explain what went wrong, why it went wrong, and then stress that you're sure she can follow your suggestions to do a better job in the future.

Constructive Criticism Within a Team
It is a good idea to foster an environment in which your team can offer each other constructive criticism from time to time. Model criticism and help them learn to do it themselves. You may need to discipline someone who offers criticism in a nonconstructive way to make your point, but a team that supports each other this way has a good chance at success.

How and where you offer constructive criticism depends on the employee and situation. It may be best to talk to some people privately. Others can handle hearing the criticism in front of the team. Think about the person you're dealing with and what may work best for him.

If you think there is value in offering up the criticism as a more general team suggestion, don't do it at the moment it happens. Instead, save it and offer it to the team in general at a team meeting without pointing out the person involved.

WHEN DISCIPLINE IS APPROPRIATE

Discipline is appropriate when an employee keeps doing the same thing wrong even after you've given him constructive criticism. It's also appropriate when a one-time incident occurs that is so serious you have to step in and take action.

When you have a problem with an employee, discipline will remove any gray area from the communication. If there has been any question about what you wanted or needed, discipline will resolve those questions because it forcefully and clearly spells out what is wrong and what has to change.

Some bad apples do not respond well to criticism until there is a consequence attached to it. These employees need discipline instead of criticism so that it's clear to them that they need to change their behavior or actions. You need to be careful not to overuse discipline. If you give written warnings for slight infractions, you're left with no choice but to escalate to probation or a pay cut if the situation happens again.

HOW TO OFFER DISCIPLINE

When you need to discipline an employee, it is important that you approach the situation in a calm and matter-of-fact way. While it can be appropriate to express your disappointment at the way the employee has behaved or handled something, this is not an opportunity for you to vent. This also isn't a time to be vague about what the employee is being disciplined for. Instead, explain what consequence you're implementing and what exactly it is in response to.

LANGUAGE

When you speak to an employee whom you're disciplining, you need to be clear, brief, and to the point. The entire conversation needs to be kept on a professional level. You're using discipline to effect a change in the employee. To get that result you need to be crystal clear as to what the problem is, what your intent is, and what action you are taking.

apples to apples A CASE STUDY

Charise needed to place Giovanna on probation, but felt bad doing so. Instead of simply giving Giovanna the facts and the consequence, she went into a long explanation about what a great job Giovanna was doing in other areas, before quickly telling her at the end of the conversation that she was on probation for having an inappropriate outgoing voicemail message that offended a client. Giovanna left the conversation scratching her head. If she was so great at everything else, the probation didn't seem to make sense. Be sure to stick to the task at hand and don't muddy the waters by discussing other aspects of the employee's performance.

Ambiguous: You'd better not keep filing this wrong. I'm going to watch and if it happens again I'll have to do something about it.

Clear: Since this is the third time in the last month I couldn't find the Acme file because you did not file it correctly, I'm placing you on thirty-day probation. This is a critical component of your job and if you misfile it again during that time, I'll be forced to end your employment with our company.

It's important that you instill ownership of the problem with the employee whenever possible. Don't take it on yourself. When you say, "I'm sorry, but I feel like I have to write you up for this," you're not placing blame on the employee. But when you say, "Your actions have given me no choice but to write you up," you make it clear that the employee brought this situation on herself.

CHASTISE IN PRIVATE

When you need to discipline an employee, the best plan is always to do so in private. If you belittle or call someone out in front of her peers, it will not improve his attitude or performance. More likely, he will become bitter and make the situation worse.

Don't Make Empty Threats

It's important that you follow through on what you tell an employee while disciplining her. If you tell Pat that the next time she makes the same mistake you're going to write her up, and she makes the mistake but you don't write her up, you've shown that your discipline is hollow. You can't expect your employees to follow through on changing their behavior or performance if you don't follow through on your own management.

Sometimes you have to make an example of an employee in front of others, but these situations are rare. For example, if Craig always brings up negatives in meetings and you have spoken to him privately about it before, but he does it again, it is appropriate for you to say, "We've talked about this and I don't want to hear any more negatives from you (or anyone else) at these meetings. Let's move on." In a situation like this, you want to be short and sweet. Say what you need to say and then move everyone past it. If you need to further discipline Craig, talk with him in private.

It may also be necessary to publicly discipline an employee to create an example. If you have a team full of people who don't seem to understand that they need to be at their desks by 9 A.M., publicly calling out the worst offender can help put the others back in line.

DEALING WITH FALLOUT

When making the decision to discipline a bad apple, it's important to understand the ramifications for that employee and for your team as a whole.

The employee you're dealing with has a limited range of choices in response to your action. He could, of course, react positively (and that's your hope), but he could also leave, make things worse, act out, take out his frustration on team members, take legal action, try to make trouble for you, or sit back and wait to be fired. Once you've reached the point with an employee where discipline is necessary, you're at the point where you've decided that things either need to change or this person needs to go. So, in this scenario, if the person quits, it's no loss. If he continues to behave inappropriately, or changes his behavior to do something different, but just as bad, it's a clear signal to you that termination is your only option.

The situation with this employee can also affect the rest of your team. If an action is taken against an employee and everyone knows about it (firing, suspension, etc.), it's likely that you'll need to address what has happened with the rest of your team. You can't share the details of the situation, but if Tina is fired for cause, you should at least tell your team what happened. If you don't, they're going to wonder and rumors will fly.

> ### Avoiding Favoritism in Discipline
> Sometimes it is necessary to discipline a good apple who just made a bad mistake. It can be tempting to let it slide since you know this person is generally dependable and a hard worker. However, you must be sure to treat like transgressions in a like way. If Anthony is an accounts payable clerk and incorrectly paid a vendor three weeks ago but only got a slap on the wrist because you know he's generally a good employee, it would be wrong to dock Sarah (a difficult employee) a day's pay for incorrectly paying an employee when she did the payroll.

It is also a good idea for you to take the situation and paint it as you want it to appear. If you want the situation to be a warning or a lesson for the rest of the team, then offer it to them that way. "I had to fire Greg today because of problems following up with clients. This is critical for everyone on our team and I will not tolerate anyone who doesn't appreciate how important it is to follow up on the leads you've been given."

DEALING WITH YOUR OWN FEELINGS ABOUT DISCIPLINE

Discipline is one of the hardest things to do as a manager. Sometimes you tell yourself that if you had been a better manager you wouldn't have reached this point with your employee. The reality is that, no matter how skilled a manager you are, some employees simply don't do what they should or behave as you expect (especially if you're dealing with a bad apple).

To feel good about the decision you've made, make sure you've taken every constructive approach before you reach the discipline stage for ongoing situations (a serious one-time incident needs immediate discipline—there's no time for constructive criticism).

If you make sure that what you're going to do is fair, it will be easier to do it. If you have reservations about how to handle the situation, take time to examine your options before taking action.

Some managers feel very uncomfortable disciplining employees. They might feel tentative, nervous, unsure, uneasy about confrontation, or simply guilty for having to speak to another person in an authoritative way that may cause the other person to feel bad. If you're in this situation, talk to yourself a little bit about the situation. Remind yourself of all the reasons this person needs to be disciplined. Think about what the consequences would be if you let the behavior continue. Remind yourself of your duty to your company. If you feel very uncomfortable with confrontation, rehearse what you are going to say and do. Meet with the person and say your piece. Move things along so there is no opportunity for backtalk or explanations. Do what you've set out to do and then get out of the situation.

Another way to feel better about the situation is to look at the impact that one difficult employee is having on the rest of your team. Instead of thinking about the feelings of that one employee, focus on how the action you are about to take will have a positive impact on the other ten people on your team.

Some managers worry that the employee will cry, get upset, or make a fuss. They feel unprepared to deal with those possibilities. If you know the employee well, you can probably predict how she will react and can prepare yourself for the scene that will ensue. In this situation, again, you want to make the meeting as short and to the point as possible. Don't allow time for emotions to build and overflow. Plow through what you have to say and then end the meeting.

PAPER TRAIL

When you discipline employees, everything has to be documented —either formally as part of the HR process or in your personnel files. It's important to keep good records both to protect yourself and to maintain a clear picture of what has happened and what action has been taken. Record the details of the incident, actions, penalties, any review, probation information, and any written statements the employee has included in paperwork.

CHAPTER 10

DITCHING
BAD APPLES

There may come a time when you feel as if you've reached the point where you'd like to (or need to) fire one of your bad apple employees. Terminations are one of the hardest parts of being a manager (even with the most difficult employees), but they can be easier if you know how to work through the situation.

CH 5. Motivating Bad Apples to Become Good

CH 6. Maintaining Good Apples

CH 7. Dealing with Personality Conflicts

CH 8. Cultivating Conflict Resolution Skills

CH 9. Disciplining Bad Apples

CH 10. Ditching Bad Apples

CH 11. Considering Legal Ramifications

HOW TO DETERMINE WHEN TO PULL THE PLUG

Making the decision to let someone go is a difficult one, no matter the circumstances. You may feel terrible when you have to let a good apple go because of restructuring, financial problems, or other reasons that were not caused by the employee, but terminating a bad apple is also difficult. As bad as your employee may be, we all know that finding candidates, interviewing candidates, calling references, and hiring and training someone is very disruptive to your own workflow and to that of your team. When you reach a point in which you have to let a bad employee go, you've reached the "tipping point"— the moment when you realize there are more negatives than positives about this employee, or when a single incident happens that makes you realize you simply cannot continue to employ this person.

When you have given an employee warnings and opportunities to change his behavior and your final warning indicates that if he doesn't make the necessary changes, you'll fire him, you have to follow through and fire him. Just as with discipline, it's important that you mean what you say and follow through on it.

REASONS TO FIRE SOMEONE

When you boil it down, there is only one reason to fire someone—their behavior or performance has somehow significantly negatively affected the company or team's productivity, prospects, corporate culture, or output. There are hundreds of things that can cause this to happen, and each one of them is a potential reason to fire someone.

Before you make this decision, you need to be sure that whatever the bad apple is doing is somehow a detriment to your company or team and is more of a problem than an asset. You need to weigh the person's skills, behavior, performance, abilities, problems, and potential and decide whether the total assessment is negative or positive. You also need to consider your ability to replace that person.

Reading Employee E-mail

As you are making the decision whether or not to fire someone, you may decide to read their company e-mail to find out how they are handling interactions with other employees, vendors, and clients. Employees do not have an expectation of privacy in company e-mail (and most companies have a clear policy that states this). While you have the right to look at employee e-mail at any time, most managers prefer to have a stated policy that lets employees know this could happen before they do so.

Some managers delay firing a person who needs to go because they can't find the courage, feel too guilty, or fool themselves into believing that something will change. If you have an employee who needs to go, the sooner you do it, the better it will be for everyone. Having that bad apple on board pulls your whole team down. Firing isn't easy, but once you do it, the negative influence on your team will be gone and you'll find that everyone is able to work better. The sooner you fire, the sooner you can move on.

If you are reluctant to fire someone, it may help to think about what would happen if one of your employees quit tomorrow. If this happened, you would find a way to make do until you could find a replacement. You and your team will always find a way to get the work done and keep things moving if a person leaves or is fired. It is rare that a person is completely essential to the company's work. Thinking about this scenario may make it easier for you to move ahead.

WHEN TO FIRE SOMEONE

Once you reach the tipping point with an employee, you most likely want to do the termination as quickly as possible, but there are some things to take into consideration. It is usually best to wait a day if it is not an emergency situation that requires immediate termination. You'll need to coordinate with your HR department so that the appropriate paperwork can be completed and you'll also need to take some time to understand all of the projects, clients, and work that employee is involved with, and create a transition plan.

If you think an employee is heading down the road to termination, but isn't quite at that point yet, it is wise to consider the projects and work that are being assigned to her. If a new project is scheduled to take eight months and you've mentally decided to give Tiara a month to see if she improves, it doesn't make sense to assign that project to her while you're still on the fence about her progress.

WHEN YOU SHOULD PUT UP AND SHUT UP

There are times when, although you want to fire someone, you shouldn't. As we've discussed earlier, sometimes you don't have the option of firing a bad apple because she has connections within the company, is tied to a key account, has a specialized skill set, or has information that makes it impossible to fire her. But, there are other situations when firing is also not a good choice. These include:

- A situation in which the company is about to go through major changes. A new acquisition or downsizing can mean a lot of upheaval and confusion. This is a good time to sit tight and maintain the status quo. You don't want to try to find and train someone new with these kinds of things going on. It can also be very difficult to know what kind of employee you need to hire if the company is undergoing changes—once the transition has happened, you may find that, instead of replacing your customer service representative, hiring another assistant makes more sense because of the new direction the company will be going.

- When you are about to leave or move up within the company. While it's not great to pass on a bad apple to your successor, it's even worse to pass along the torch and expect the new person to have to immediately hire someone to fill an empty space. Taking over a department with a gaping hole in it is very difficult.

- Your team or company is about to begin a crucial or large project and you do not have time to find a replacement. Unless the bad apple employee is going to be detrimental to the project, it is probably in your best interests to keep him on board.

- Economic reasons make it difficult or impossible to hire someone for what you are paying the current employee. If the job market has changed and people with your bad apple's qualifications are now making a lot more than you're paying, you may not be able to afford a replacement, or you may have to hire someone less skilled or experienced.

Putting up with a bad apple may not be the best situation, but in these circumstances it is often the lesser evil.

CONSEQUENCES OF FIRING BAD APPLES

Firing a bad apple has consequences for you, your team, and your company. While the termination may be necessary, you still need to be aware of the consequences and think them through before you take any action.

> **Taking Personal Lives into Account**
> It can be hard to know to what extent you should take an employee's personal life into account when making the decision to terminate her. If her husband just got laid off from his job and you know that firing her will completely decimate them, you'll likely have a hard time making this decision. However, while you are human, there are times when you cannot wait for a person's situation to stabilize. You can try to wait and give the person a chance to get to a better place personally, but be aware that some personal crises go on for long periods of time. If her husband is still unemployed in three months, it's simply not reasonable for you to hold off on the firing. You must do what is right for the company.

When you fire someone, one of the biggest consequences that you face is the potential loss of other employees. If your team members believe that the action you took was fair, you have a better chance of keeping them. When you fire a bad apple, often you won't need to say much—it's obvious to everyone what the problem was with this employee, so an explanation from you won't be necessary.

Sometimes the employee you let go may try to recruit team members away from you. Your employees are free to leave and follow the bad apple if they choose, but they're more likely to stay if you help them understand that they are valued and appreciated on your team.

Letting a bad apple go may have a positive impact on your team. They may see that the dead weight is gone and come to work with a better attitude. They may become more involved in their jobs, create a better work atmosphere, and strengthen their team relationship.

Firing this employee may allow you the opportunity to make changes to the way things are done by your team or to alter the approach your team takes to some projects or situations. Take this opportunity to talk with your team about processes and procedures. They may have suggestions they didn't have before or didn't feel comfortable expressing while the bad apple was part of the team. Seeing someone leave may help them view the team in a new light.

Firing a BFF

If you have two employees who are best friends and you have to fire one of them, you can expect some backlash from the remaining employee. It's best to talk to her separately and give her the big picture reason for the firing (again, you cannot get into details). Emphasize her own value to the team and share with her where the team will be going from here. Offer positive feedback about her work. Doing so may lessen the chance she will quit. You also need to make sure she doesn't pass any confidential information to the fired employee and you should talk with her about your company's policy regarding this.

Let your team know whether you will be replacing the employee who has been fired. If you won't be replacing him, let the team know how work will be redistributed to make up for the loss of a teammate. Be sure to not minimize the impact on the team. Acknowledge that this change will have an effect on them. You can say things like, "I know this puts all of you in a tough spot, but I'm confident that we're going to be able to do what needs to be done." Being honest about this change may have an impact on the speed with which projects are moved through the team. Be realistic about things and make it clear that you are adjusting your expectations for the new situation. Wherever possible, you want the team to know that you're going to be involved in getting the work done and help to minimize the impact of the situation. If you expect them to complete the same amount of work in the same amount of time, you're going to create one stressed-out team, which is a breeding ground for more bad apples.

Another possible consequence from a termination has to do with clients. If the bad apple you fired had a good relationship with a client, you may be in danger of losing that client. To minimize this risk, reach out to that employee's clients immediately. Reassure the clients. Explain that some changes have been made and their contact is no longer with the company. Introduce the clients to the new contact and reassure them that you'll make sure that the change has as little impact as possible on their company. Really sell the new contact to the clients—tout his expertise and abilities. Make yourself available to the clients during the transition for any questions or concerns. In a way, you have to resell the account at this point, but protecting against the possibility of lost revenue makes this important.

The termination may also have an impact on other managers. If the terminated employee worked with another manager's team, that manager is understandably going to be concerned. Help the other manager understand the reasons for the firing. Have a plan in place to deal with the transition and reassure the other manager that you will strive to keep the impact on his team as small as possible.

HOW TO FIRE SOMEONE

Knowing that you need to fire someone and actually doing it are two different things. Many managers aren't sure about the "right" way to terminate a bad apple.

Get any paperwork done before you meet with the employee to give him the news. You want to make sure that you've done everything required by your HR department and that all forms are completed and ready to go. Once you contact HR and the circle of people who know about the firing grows, you need to move forward with the termination as quickly as possible since the possibility of a leak increases.

When you talk to the employee being terminated, it's important that you control your tone and demeanor. You need to lay things out in a straightforward way. Don't stall or beat around the bush. The employee may know you're there to tell her she's fired (if you've had ongoing discussions and attempts at improving behavior or performance and they have failed, it won't be much of a surprise) and prolonging the agony doesn't help anyone. Be sure that you look her in the eyes without wavering. Don't allow her to intimidate you.

Be very clear and simply tell her that you are terminating her employment immediately. Give her information about the basic reasons. Collect any company property she has before you give her the last paycheck, if it's been generated, and any paperwork required by HR. (Note: You should place a list of company property that's in the employee's possession in her file with both her signature and yours on it when possession is first given, so there is no question about what must be returned.)

Do not apologize for having to fire the person. When you terminate an employee for misconduct or failure to perform, you have nothing to apologize for and you shouldn't imply that you do. It is fine to have a gentle tone or a softer demeanor to show you have empathy for what the person is feeling, but be clear there is nothing to argue about and that you're not there to be convinced otherwise. Allow her time to speak, but don't allow her to sway you from your position. Answer any questions that you feel you can, but don't answer those that:

- You don't feel comfortable answering
- You do not know the answer to
- Have to do with protected company information
- Have legal ramifications

Final Paycheck

In some states, your company must give the employee her last paycheck within a number of hours if you fire her. Check with your HR department about what rules apply to you so you can give the employee the correct information.

For example:

Answer: Do I get paid for my unused vacation time?
Don't answer: Are you going to be replacing me?
Answer: Will I have health insurance?
Don't answer: Is this because I'm pregnant?

Once you have answered (or deflected) all the questions, end the meeting as quickly as possible.

If you are firing an employee who is known to be very troublesome, it is a good idea to have another manager present when you fire her so that there is a witness in case she blows her top.

Once an employee has been terminated, allow him to clean out his desk (if he cannot be trusted or is in a volatile state, you can have him removed from the premises and have his things returned to him later). He should then be asked to leave. No matter how friendly things are or how much you trust him, don't give him the opportunity to take confidential information, interact much with other employees, tamper with company equipment or files, or make trouble in general. A swift exit is the safest way to protect the company's interests. In some companies, the policy is that all terminated employees are escorted to their desks and then escorted from the building. If this is the case for you, make sure a box is ready for the employee's personal belongings.

You'll want to alert the IT department about the termination so that they can immediately turn off that employee's access to the network, files, and company e-mail. If the employee has personal files or information on the work computer, you have the option of allowing him time to remove them with supervision, or to have the IT department handle it. Note that most companies have a policy that all information stored on company computers belongs to the company.

Here's a list of other things to do once you terminate a bad apple:

- Conduct an exit interview or confirm who within your company will conduct it
- Change all of his passwords (as well as any generally used company or network passwords) and get any keys or passcards back

- Revoke any signature power she has at the bank for the company
- Get a final expense report from the employee and make sure it is paid
- Cancel or change any company credit cards he had access to
- Confirm that HR is handling health insurance issues
- Change the company literature and website to remove his name
- Reroute his calls or give his cell phone to someone else

MANAGING YOUR OWN FEELINGS

Firing someone is never easy. In addition to following the procedures laid out by your company, you also have your own emotions to deal with. This can be challenging—no one feels good about firing someone, even if the person you're firing is a bad apple.

EMOTIONS DURING FIRING

When you have to fire someone, you may start to feel stressed out once the decision is made. It may be a relief to know this person will no longer be a problem; however, actually telling someone to her face that she's being terminated is a tough thing to do.

Before the meeting, remind yourself of all the reasons why the person needs to go. Tell yourself that you're doing the right thing and that you gave the bad apple every chance to make this work. Remember your responsibility to the rest of the team and to the company.

Some managers are reluctant to fire people and put it off to avoid the confrontation. This may seem like a good way to avoid conflict, but it actually ends up making the conflict worse. If your employee makes the same mistake over and over and over and you don't fire him, it's the same as telling him that his mistake is acceptable. If you suddenly fire him for the same mistake he's been making for the past four months, he's going to be shocked and probably upset, creating an even bigger confrontation than if you had just fired him after he failed to correct his mistake after the first few warnings.

Don't soften the firing. Remain firm. Keep your composure during the conversation. Some managers find it's very emotional to fire someone and feel as though they may cry while doing it. You can't let that happen. It's fine to have empathy, but you have to remain in control and in charge. You also need to keep your composure so you aren't baited into an argument. Some terminated employees get angry and start making accusations or delivering insults. And some bad apples may react to the situation with exaggerated bad behavior simply because that is part of their personality. Remain calm. Say that you understand the employee is upset, but that the meeting is over.

Some managers find themselves getting angry during the firing and want to say things such as, "You're making me fire you. I don't like to do this and it's your fault." Keep your cool. It's okay to be angry, but you shouldn't express it in this meeting.

During the firing don't react to the negative feedback you get from the employee, but make some room for reflection upon it afterward. There may be some merit in what the person said to you. If Tana says that if you'd given her better instructions when you hired her, she wouldn't be in this position, there may be a grain of truth to that. It's not your fault she is being fired (if she needed better instructions she certainly could have asked for them), however, perhaps you could offer clearer instructions in the future.

EMOTIONS AFTER THE FACT

Firing a bad apple can be a difficult situation for you, as a manager, to handle. You may wonder if you really did all you could do to keep this employee or to help her to change. You might feel horrible at the idea of taking a job away from someone who really needs it.

Keep in mind that, as a manager, you're a representative for your company. If firing this person is what's best for the company, then it is your responsibility to do it. It wasn't your responsibility to handhold this employee or put up with bad work. Sometimes people just don't work out, particularly if the person in question is a bad apple.

It's also common for a manager who is firing someone to worry about her, even if it is an employee he didn't like. Losing a job can be quite a blow to a person's self-esteem, not to mention that it puts her in a difficult economic position. Again, it's good to feel empathy—it means you're human. It also means that you're not taking this decision lightly and are weighing the needs of the company against the needs of the individual employee, which is what you are paid to do. You can't wallow in guilt about the decision once you've taken action. The employee is an adult who is responsible for her own life. If she couldn't do this job, then she'll have to find another.

Outsourcing

Outsourcing is an option to consider when you are making a transition plan for a fired employee. Outsourcing some or all of that employee's work is a great way to keep work flowing while you seek a permanent replacement. Some managers choose to permanently outsource some of their team's work.

It takes some time to get over the emotions involved with a firing. Make sure you have a plan in place that will help you and your team move forward, so that you're not sitting in your office beating yourself up two days from now.

You need to keep your emotions from having an impact on your team. It's okay (and good) for your employees to see you are not heartless and that firing someone isn't easy for you. However, you don't want your team to think that you're weak or have a hard time making these decisions. You're responsible for setting the tone for your team. If you're miserable, they'll question your decision. You also need to be sure you don't badmouth the employee to the rest of the team. This will make them wonder what you might say about them. You don't want the team to think that badmouthing other people is acceptable or encouraged, so don't allow them to do it either.

QUITTING

When a bad apple employee quits, you may feel a great sense of relief. He's leaving and you didn't have to fire him. However, there are still concerns and things you should pay attention to in this situation.

"I QUIT"

When a bad apple employee quits just before you are about to fire her, she may be doing so to save face. It's fine to allow her this comfort. One concern that may come up is whether she should give two weeks' notice. Most employees will give you two weeks' notice when they quit (and your employee handbook may require this). If someone is bad enough that you planned to fire her, it's unlikely you want her hanging around for two weeks, poisoning the other employees, or possibly messing up projects.

If you feel comfortable enough with this employee and believe she can work responsibly for the two weeks, you can accept the notice. However, if you don't feel she can be trusted and aren't comfortable monitoring her for that long, you don't have to accept the notice (again, unless the company handbook says otherwise). You can tell her that you don't need her to stay that long and agree on a shorter time period. Usually, if she's quitting, she's got another job lined up and will be happy to get out sooner.

If an employee quits, your company does not have to pay unemployment insurance.

"YOU'RE FIRED." "NO, I QUIT."

When you terminate a bad apple he may become angry and not accept the situation. He may insist you're not firing him and that he's quitting. The only situation in which this will make a difference is when it comes to unemployment insurance. If you fire him first and he is eligible for unemployment, he can make a claim. If he says, "You don't need to fire me. I'll give you my resignation," you can agree that you are accepting his resignation. Be sure to document what has happened though, so that if he does file for unemployment, you have some proof of exactly what transpired.

Ditching a bad apple, whether you've fired her or she's left on her own, can leave you with a mix of emotions. However, no matter what scenario you encounter, you want to keep the legal ramifications for both you and your employee in mind.

CHAPTER 11

CONSIDERING LEGAL RAMIFICATIONS

Although a lot of managing has to do with going with your gut feeling, it's important to understand what your rights and responsibilities are as a manager. When dealing with troublesome employees (who may be more likely to file lawsuits or point fingers), you should understand how to best protect yourself and your company while also managing your employees to the best of your ability. This chapter is designed to give you a general summary so you can recognize issues, and is not a substitute for expert HR involvement or legal advice.

CH 5. Motivating Bad Apples to Become Good

CH 6. Maintaining Good Apples

CH 7. Dealing with Personality Conflicts

CH 8. Cultivating Conflict Resolution Skills

CH 9. Disciplining Bad Apples

CH 10. Ditching Bad Apples

CH 11. Considering Legal Ramifications

YOUR COMPANY POLICIES

It's important that your company has written policies (such as an employee handbook) that employees must follow. Your manual should have explicit disclaimers in the front, the terms of which may vary from state to state, making clear that the manual is not a contract with employees, and that the employer reserves its employment-at-will rights. However, the manual does serve as a conduct guide for employees, and may make it easier to explain the reason for a termination to an employee.

The disclaimer at the front of the manual usually reserves the right to amend anything in the manual. It is a good idea to have an employee sign an acknowledgement of any changes to the policy, as well certifying receipt of the manual itself. A number of companies now have them in electronic format.

LIABILITY

One concern with bad apples is the liability they expose your company to. If the bad apple employee makes a mistake that causes your company to be sued, your company could be on the line for a lot of damages. Because of this, you want to remove a bad apple employee as soon as possible to reduce your company's liability.

WARNINGS

There are no legal requirements about how or when to create written warnings for employees, unless your company's employee manual sets out a specific procedure or requirements. However, a warning can be a key piece of evidence if there is ever an employment lawsuit with someone you fire. The first thing a government agency will ask your company is: "Let me see your documentation."

A key way to give notice of and attempt to change inadequate performance or behavior is to do regular evaluations. Set up a schedule and stick to it. During these evaluations you can talk about any problems you see developing. This is your chance to steer your bad apple in a better direction. These evaluations also provide documentation that you've discussed problems and keep track of what kinds of solutions or plans of action you've agreed on together. In order to track progress, create goals and timetables for their accomplishment—and then follow up.

Some companies prefer that their managers give a verbal warning before any written warnings are given, depending upon the offense in question. If you give a verbal warning, be sure to document it in the file. A written warning can be used if behavior or performance does not improve, or if things worsen. These warnings should be issued when the incident happens. When you document an incident, you want to be sure to include:

- The date
- The names of those involved
- A brief description of the problem (so that you and anyone not familiar with the situation can easily understand what happened)
- A description of exactly what the plan is, with details about milestone dates and performance specifics that are expected
- Notice that more severe discipline, up to and including termination, will be implemented if there is a repeat of the behavior
- The employee's signature on the formal warning paperwork, indicating it was received (thought not necessarily that the employee agrees with any part of it). If the employee refuses to sign, make a notation to that effect

There is a fine line to walk with warnings and writeups. On one hand, you can't write up your employees for every single minor event. If you're dealing with a bad apple, the constant negative reinforcement may not help improve behavior (if Shay has a negative attitude and you write him up and berate him for every negative comment, you're not going to make a lot of progress with him). Also, if you write up every single thing and there is an employment lawsuit later on, it could look like you were calculating a way to fire this person.

On the other hand, a far bigger problem is that too many managers fail to make records of warnings. If you document them, you have a clear path if you decide that you need to fire that bad apple. If you are working with someone who is particularly difficult, you want to be sure that you've dotted your *I*s and crossed your *T*s.

PROBATION

Probation is a period of time in which an employee has to show improvement or progress, during which he is closely monitored. Probation can be used in two different ways. One type of probation is when you hire a new employee and he is placed on probation for a short period at the beginning of his employment so that you can monitor his work. Another kind of probation is when you place an existing employee on probation because of a problem you've encountered. The idea behind both types of probation is that if the employee doesn't successfully complete the probation, he'll be terminated.

When you place someone on probation, it is key that you clarify in writing what the terms of the probation are and what he has to do to complete the probation successfully. Lay out how the employee will be monitored and how and when you will evaluate progress throughout the process.

Probation does not diminish an employee's rights when it comes to federal and state employment discrimination and harassment laws, but you'll have put your best foot forward by giving the employee a chance to improve and a clear warning as to the consequences of not improving.

Do regular evaluations with your employee during the probationary period so that you can closely track her progress or problems during this time period.

SUSPENSIONS

There are two types of workplace suspensions—disciplinary and nondisciplinary, or investigatory, suspensions. A disciplinary suspension occurs when you suspect an employee of a single incident or a pattern of behavior or misconduct. A nondisciplinary suspension may be appropriate while investigating a complaint, charge, or problem, particularly when a claim of sexual harassment has been made. Typically, investigatory suspensions are without pay, except in the public (government) sector. For private sector employment, retroactive pay is usually given once the employee in question is cleared of any wrongdoing.

A suspension is also a good way to get someone out of the workplace so you can have some time to find out what has really happened. It can also be useful when there is a major dispute between two people and they need some space to cool down. Suspensions are disruptive to the team however, so use them only when necessary. Some suspensions can actually make the situation worse. If Jill is regularly late to work and her absence is making it impossible for the team to get work done, suspending her is simply going to make things worse for your team. In this kind of situation, you should rely on other types of discipline.

FIRING

Terminating an employee is always a hard decision. It's important that you handle terminations properly to minimize any problems for you or your company.

You will need to be careful you do not violate any discrimination laws when you fire someone. It is illegal to fire someone because he or she:

- Is over the age of forty
- Has been called up for military service
- Has a disability
- Is a certain race, color, religion, sex, or national origin
- Is pregnant
- Has supported a union
- Protested safety issues
- Made complaints about prior pay

Some states have expanded on the federal law and make it illegal to fire people for things such as marital status and sexual orientation. You also cannot fire an employee as retaliation for him reporting a violation at the company (whistle blowing) or for refusing to do something that violates state policy.

You do have the right to fire any employee for any legal reason, unless the employee handbook states that you cannot fire someone without good cause or if a special procedure must be followed prior to a termination. This is known as the "employment at will" doctrine, but you should be aware that many states have a number of exceptions to it. Also, if that employee has a written employment agreement, or is covered under a union contract, you usually can't fire the person without good cause. It's a good idea that you, as a manager, talk with your HR department to understand what, if any, restrictions exist on terminations within your team and company.

A good rule of thumb is to only fire someone when that is what is best for the company. If his behavior, performance, interactions, or production negatively affects the company or its bottom line, you're firing the person for the right reason. Pressuring an employee to resign can legally be the same thing as firing him, but sometimes it makes sense to come to an agreement that the employee will resign instead of being fired.

Severance pay is an issue that is dictated by your company's policy and is something that can be negotiated. Many times, severance pay is offered in exchange for a signed waiver by the employee that states that she isn't going to attempt to sue the company for employment discrimination or wrongful termination. If your company already has a severance policy in place, you can't require an employee to sign this type of waiver to receive the severance.

Government Employees

The rules are a bit different when you work for the government. You can't fire someone for their political beliefs or membership in clubs and associations. You can't fire an employee for using his freedom of speech on a general topic of public interest (the rule is different when speech is related to the job). Most government employees are covered by due process, which means you have to give notice of the reason for termination and the opportunity for a hearing.

There is no requirement that you must give an employee that you are terminating two weeks' notice (unless there is a union agreement, contract, or employee handbook stating this is required). Sometimes you may feel as though giving the employee notice of the termination is a nice thing to do (so he can find another job and make some financial arrangements). Unfortunately, what seems like the "nice" thing to do is probably not the right thing to do in terms of what is best for your company. An employee who knows he is being fired is unlikely to do much work while waiting for the ax to fall and, in fact, may decide to take some actions that are harmful to the company.

If you are tempted to let the terminated employee train her replacement, don't! She's likely to pass on her bad attitude, bad habits, or bad information.

Don't Say What You Don't Know

When talking to an employee you are terminating, don't make representations about things that are not within your area of responsibility or knowledge. If you make promises or guarantees to the employee your company could be held to them. Areas you should not comment on include:

- 401(k)s and retirement plans
- Health insurance
- Severance pay
- Disability insurance
- Flexible Spending Accounts (FSAs)
- Eligibility for unemployment insurance

In many cases, it is best if you fire an employee at the end of a chain of documented warnings, unless the offense is so huge that it requires immediate termination. You'll have a file full of written documentation that eventually led to the firing. In this kind of situation, you've not only given the employee every opportunity to improve his performance, but you've also created a paper trail that will be helpful should the employee decide to sue for wrongful termination.

> **Health Insurance**
> Under the federal COBRA law, your employee has the right to continue his health insurance by paying the premium amount himself, except in rare circumstances of gross misconduct. Your HR department should generate the paperwork for this and provide him with rates and deadlines. The employer may also charge a 2 percent administrative fee.

If you must fire an employee immediately, without any background problems (such as you catch her stealing from the company, find him involved in a fight on the premises, or other serious infractions), it makes sense to take a deep breath, get all the facts, and get some backup. You may even consider an investigatory suspension while you gather information. Get your boss on the scene, or at least another manager. Collect information about any witnesses to the event and make sure another manager is present when you terminate the employee.

AVOIDING UNEMPLOYMENT INSURANCE DISPUTES

Unemployment insurance is a state-run program that allows for a percentage (usually about 60 percent) of a person's pay for a number of weeks (usually twenty-six) after being terminated from a job. Its purpose is to help people who lose their jobs survive financially while looking for other jobs. While this is a great program for employees, it can be very expensive for the employer. The company's rates are based on how many claims it has had in the last year. Because of this, your employer may want you to try to limit the situations in which unemployment insurance is needed.

As a general rule, an employee can collect unemployment insurance when his termination does not involve gross misconduct. If the employee quits, he has no right to unemployment, unless a reasonable person in his situation would also quit because of the situation or conditions. Basic dissatisfaction is not enough.

Employees terminated for gross misconduct are not entitled to unemployment benefits. Depending on local law, gross misconduct may include:

- Attendance problems, particularly when there is no reasonable excuse for the absences or when the employee was absent without notice
- Insubordination
- Theft
- Harassment
- Falsification of company records
- Fighting or threats of violence

References

If you fire an employee and you get a call checking references about that person, the best thing to do is say little at all. While you may want to warn the other employer about this bad apple, instead say that you can only verify the dates of employment, position held, and if you receive a document asking to verify a specific rate of pay, that you will state whether you can confirm or deny that. State that this is your company's policy. Say nothing else about the employee. This protects you from a possible defamation suit.

If you fire an employee but the reasons were minor, he will likely be entitled to unemployment insurance.

PROPER DOCUMENTATION

Documentation is the key to any employment situation when it comes to legal disputes. It's very important that your company has a procedure set up for documenting warnings, suspensions, probations, and terminations. However, having a procedure means nothing if you don't actually follow it. One of the less glamorous aspects of a management job is the paperwork. It falls to you to document all of these events that occur with your employees. Good documentation is not as simple as it sounds. Include the following:

- Dates
- Names
- Exact description of the action taken
- A brief, accurate description of what led to this event, including dates and names
- Information about any witnesses to the event that led to the action, or any witnesses to your conversation about the action you are taking

PART 3

FEND OFF FUTURE **BAD** APPLES

CHAPTER 12

CREATE A POSITIVE WORK ENVIRONMENT

There are many things you can do to create an environment that not only encourages good apples, but discourages bad apple behavior. As a manager, you really do have a lot of influence over how your employees feel about their jobs and how they behave at work.

CH 12. Create a Positive Work Environment

CH 13. Avoid Hiring Bad Apples

CONCLUSION Balancing the Apple Cart

TEAM CULTURE

The team culture is the most important influence on your employees. The team culture is a general attitude or mood that permeates your group of employees and influences the way they approach work and feel about their jobs. Sometimes the team culture is the same as the corporate culture, but in some circumstances it can be different. Team culture develops gradually and can be difficult to change.

Team culture is influenced by many factors, including the workplace atmosphere, your management style, and individual team member personalities. If your company has multiple divisions and locations, each group will develop its own feel and approach. It can be good to encourage these distinctions, but you don't want any one group to feel superior, isolated, or totally self-reliant.

You can help cultivate a positive team culture in many ways:

- Allow a common area to be decorated with signs, posters, paint, and more that the team collectively agrees on
- Allow team members to use nicknames (appropriate ones) to identify themselves to each other within interoffice communications
- Engage in team meetings that focus on brainstorming ways to improve the way the team functions together

All of these help bring a team together. A positive team culture is important, especially when employees rely on others to help them complete a task or job. The peer pressure that exists when everyone pulls together for a common goal can be very powerful and force a bad apple to acquiesce to the will of the group.

apples to apples A CASE STUDY

Manager Kathy's company is participating in an upcoming trade show and Lisa is responsible for preparing the kits that will be handed out at their booth. She's swamped and will have a hard time meeting the shipping deadline to ensure they arrive in time. Ben is reluctant to help Lisa since he feels it's not his job and has nothing to do with him, but Bob, Rebecca, and Steve all agree to stay late each night for a week to help out. They all form an assembly line the first night, but realize one more set of hands would make things go more smoothly. The team then applies some good-natured pressure on Ben, who, once he sees that everyone else is pitching in and that he has been singled out as the bad apple, agrees to help out.

The kits ship on time and Kathy sends a personal e-mail to everyone, including Ben, thanking them for their terrific effort and teamwork. Ben, in turn, thanks the others for convincing him to help out and begins to appreciate the value that comes from working as a team. Kathy's e-mail has reinforced the necessity for and value of teamwork and has helped her narcissist see that it truly does pay to think of others. Ben, who was a potential bad apple, has been steered in the other direction because he has come to value teamwork.

A positive team culture is created by the interpersonal work you do with your employees. If you project a positive attitude, make yourself available, encourage, reward their progress, and try to make work a fun and comfortable place, you'll take huge steps toward creating a good team culture. Team culture is also influenced by the way employees interact with each other. Monitor what is happening, direct team talk to positive things, and try to reduce complaining.

Another huge influence on team culture is upper management. If the employees feel that the company really cares about them, wants to create a good working place for them, and is not there to use and abuse them, the team will develop positive morale.

INTERACTIONS

Setting the right tone for interactions between employees will go a long way toward developing a positive environment. Creating an atmosphere of respect prevents bad attitudes like bullying, confrontation, and naysaying from popping up. Each employee should feel comfortable expressing himself within the group or in one-to-one interactions. All employees should use respectful language, gestures, and correspondence with other employees.

As a manager, you want to allow employees to express their ideas and comments. If you are abrupt or interrupt them when they speak, your team members will then feel that is an acceptable way to respond.

Follow these tips to create healthy team interactions:

- **Ask for input.** Encourage your employees to express themselves within the team environment. The more communication there is, the better everyone will understand each other and the work they need to do.
- **Step in when things reach the border of appropriateness.** If two people are having a discussion in a meeting, it's good to let them resolve it themselves. But if other people are getting uncomfortable, or the tone of the conversation has changed, it's time to step in and redirect.

- **Start meetings with friendly chitchat.** This can help the team see that it's okay (and good) to have friendly personal interactions with each other.
- **Show that humor has its place.** Be funny and relaxed with your team at times, but show them that it is important to be serious about work. If things get too silly, step in and redirect your team.

SETTING EXPECTATIONS

When you first become a manager or when a new employee is added, you should be sure that everyone is clear about the ground rules that apply to the team. The type of language—both verbal and written—that is expected in the workplace, as well as the general demeanor and types of interaction you expect from and between employees should be clearly defined. For example, it may sound a little basic to tell your employees that you expect them to be respectful of others, but the truth is that saying it out loud reinforces it even though everyone already knows this is a basic requirement. This also makes it easier to deal with a problem employee later. If you've specifically enunciated what is expected, you can clearly point out a problem to your bad apple, "I made it clear that everyone on the team needs to treat each other with respect and, in this instance, you certainly didn't."

Another great way to set expectations is to offer samples, checklists, and examples to your team. Creating templates or sample documents gives them a solid reference for their own work and clarifies exactly what you expect them to produce.

Be consistent in your reinforcement of the established expectations. It can be easy to ignore or overlook a comment here or a poorly worded e-mail there, but a bad apple will take advantage of this slippery slope. That's not to say that every infraction should generate a meeting or e-mail reminding the team about proper behavior. Your monitoring and response has to be tempered by the weight of the incident. For instance, you are cc'd on an e-mail to a coworker that said, "Are you stupid? Everyone knows you have to file the reports by Friday." A phone call to the offending party with some suggested improved language such as, "Next time, a simple note like 'Just a reminder that reports have to be filed by Friday,'" is sufficient.

Try to avoid these pitfalls when it comes to the expectations you hold for your employees:

- **Setting them too high.** Sure, you want your team to break previous performance records, but your expectations need to be realistic. If your expectations are too high, no one is going to feel motivated to even try to meet them.
- **Not meeting the expectations yourself.** If you have one set of rules for your workers and one for yourself, the disparity will be obvious to them.
- **Setting expectations for every minor detail.** Too many rules, regulations, or requirements can be confusing or insulting, which will result in employees ignoring them. It can also feel very restricting to employees who don't want to be treated like kindergarteners.
- **Changing them from month to month, week to week, or even day to day.** Be sure you have thought your expectations through before issuing them or requiring that they be followed. A lack of consistency will result in employees questioning when your expectations matter since they seem to constantly change. It can make you appear wishy-washy and your team will lose respect for your leadership and management.

Be sure that you have an opportunity to periodically review correspondence or participate in phone calls with clients or vendors made by your employees. Look for opportunities to comment on when they do a good job, not just when they do it poorly. Employees want to know when they are doing a good job and meeting expectations and when they are not.

TEAM BUILDING

Team building—a process that encourages employees to establish closer relationships with each other—is a way for employees to feel more connected to each other. Activities that encourage this can help reveal different aspects of people's personalities and allow people to have shared experiences. When people only see each other in an office setting, they don't get the chance to really know each other. With team building, they become more tied to one another on a personal level, and feel more invested in each other's professional success. A team that supports itself and its members will be more productive and successful. Team members who feel connected to one another come to see their team as a family of sorts and are less likely to cause problems within the "family."

It isn't always easy to get everyone to fully participate. You've probably rolled your eyes yourself at the notion of some team building activities. Pick activities that:

- **Fit your team.** For example, planning to have everyone participate in a marathon might make sense if you work at a gym, but not everyone in the customer service department at a department store would find it so inviting.
- **Are easy for everyone to participate in.** Have a fun and relaxed dessert day when all team members bring in a favorite dessert, either homemade or store bought, and spend

a half hour at lunchtime trying each other's contributions. Anyone can participate in this, no special skills or interests are required.

- **Inspire your team.** Working together to benefit a charity is a great way to get people interested and emotionally involved with each other. There are many options to choose from. You could have the team sponsor the company's involvement with a food bank, organize a book drive for inner-city schools, or donate pennies to buy mosquito nets for African countries. Have your team work together to publicize the event within the company by making signs, sending e-mail, and talking about it at company meetings. This kind of activity allows them to work together on something not related to work, but that can actually help improve the skills needed within the workplace.

- **Are respectful of their time.** Sometimes it is necessary to have a weekend off-site retreat, but most of the time, mid-level employees will be annoyed if you require them to give up a weekend. Instead, do things that don't infringe on free time, such as scheduling a two-hour speaker to come and work with your team one morning.

DEFUSING SITUATIONS

If you know that you have a difficult employee on your team, being prepared to defuse situations before they escalate will keep the team atmosphere calm and positive. Prevention is key to keeping the team working at an even pace.

Consider the physical location of employees who are prone to problems. If Taryn and Kendall are prone to picking at each other all day, positioning them farther apart (outside of earshot of each other) can help prevent a blowup from happening. If Jordan tends to bully employees when left on his own, it could be helpful to position him close to your office, where you can monitor his behavior.

Once a situation develops, act swiftly and authoritatively to prevent escalation. This doesn't mean shouting or creating a scene. It means that once you decide to intervene, you need to take some real action that will have an actual impact on solving the problem. Before taking any steps, be clear in your own mind about what you expect those involved to do. If a shouting match is going on, calmly but firmly ask everyone to be quiet and take a deep breath. If body language and other signs indicate that emotions are running high, ask Kayla to go to the small conference room, while Cerise takes a walk to the lunchroom. Don't appear to assign blame or take sides at this point. Your goal is to first calm everyone down and then focus on sorting out what happened and why.

A good manager can see a situation developing and step in before anything has really happened. That means you need to learn to read your employee's signals. Understand their patterns of behavior and how they react to each other. Physical signs that an employee is getting upset include arm crossing, pen tapping, lip biting, or eye rolling. The more agitated the employee, the more careful you need to be in defusing the situation. Another signal is voice changes. Many people talk faster, louder, or higher when they feel threatened or frustrated. You should also watch to see how your employees deal with criticism. Some employees get very defensive or almost angry when corrected by a manager or teammate. Being knowledgeable about your employees can help you defuse a situation before it starts.

MODELING GOOD BEHAVIOR

People learn by example and your team is no exception. The most important model your team has is you. If you can show them good work habits, good decision-making, quality time management, and other important skills, they'll be able to emulate you.

Some key opportunities to model include:

- Exposing team members to how you craft e-mail, make phone calls, or have meetings with clients and vendors can allow you to demonstrate professional approaches, especially in potentially touchy or sensitive engagements. Try to remember to share these moments (or at least talk about them afterward) with your team.

- Work hours. You don't always have to be the first at the office or the last to leave. Demonstrating a good work/life balance is important. Help the team to understand when you feel it is necessary to work late (for important project deadlines or an unexpected crisis), and when you don't (all the time over issues that don't warrant that type of life interruption).

- Dress. Encouraging employees to dress in a professional manner, regardless of their job title, is important. "Look sharp, feel sharp, be sharp" is not just a cliché. This doesn't mean that suits and dresses are required, but a sloppy or unkempt appearance doesn't promote good work. As the manager, you need to make the effort to appear professional at all times. However, remember that you may need to dress one level above your employees to demonstrate your level of responsibility.

Your team can also learn from its peers. It can be dangerous to always hold up an employee and say, "Look what a great job Kim is doing! If the rest of you could work this hard, we would be in a much better place," but sometimes it can be helpful to point out employees on your team and elsewhere in the company and use them as examples of great performance.

If you are trying to motivate a bad apple, find opportunities to praise her for positive things she has done (which you can use as a model for her future behavior). These should not stretch the truth, since that demeans the real progress other employees achieve. The employee will also meet false praise with cynicism because she knows she didn't do her best work. Instead, look for honest achievements or improvements that you can highlight and praise.

PHYSICAL ENVIRONMENT

While the human environment is a key component that helps people enjoy their jobs, the physical workspace environment is just as important. If people work in a clean, bright, colorful, comfortable area they're more likely to feel positive about their work and give things their all. The building you're in and some other factors are probably not within your control, but there are still a lot of things you can do to make the work area a nice one.

SPACE

Space is a very important issue. If people are crowded and feel like they're on top of each other, they're bound to be crankier than they would be if they had a little more room. If space is a problem for your team, think about how you can reconfigure the area. You may find that drawing a to-scale diagram of the area and then moving little scale cutouts of desks and equipment around the drawing will help you find configurations you may never have considered. The standard rule of thumb is to allow 160 to 250 usable square feet per person.

Flexible scheduling can also help with space issues. If you can stagger employee start and end times, it will decrease the amount of traffic in the workplace. Be sure the way you offer flextime doesn't create an impression of favoritism within the team.

TRAFFIC FLOW

Maintaining good traffic flow throughout your team area is another way to keep the workspace feeling comfortable. If people have to maneuver around desks like a maze, you need a change. You also don't want a main highway of your company to go straight through your team. It's very distracting and can keep the team from bonding well. People who need to interact with each other regularly should be positioned close together so they can be more productive. If work orders are taken by Tonya and then need to be given to Reggie for scheduling, seat them close together so Tonya isn't getting up and walking over to Reggie's desk halfway across the office twenty times a day. Close proximity will also mean they will work together more smoothly. If Tonya has to walk across the office to give Reggie the orders, she might decide to only do it twice a day, which could result in the scheduling taking longer.

You need to understand patterns of traffic within your team's area. If there are busy times when other company employees must be in your area, for example when drivers have to pick up their list of deliveries for the day between 8:30 A.M. and 9:00 A.M., don't try to schedule team meetings at that time.

NOISE CONTROL

Another consideration is noise annoyance, such as vehicle traffic near windows and doors, electronically generated noise like faxes, printers, scanners, telephone conversations that are overheard and so on. This kind of noise can be very distracting to some workers. Make note of the noise level in your office and try to minimize the impact of extraneous noise whenever possible.

Many companies also have music playing over ceiling speakers or even through their phone systems. This sounds like a great idea, but in reality it often doesn't work. Everyone has different tastes and what you find relaxing, your employees may find annoying. Instrumental music may be the safest choice depending on your clients and workers. If you pipe music through the phone system to each desk, make sure the employee has the option of turning it off at his desk.

EQUIPMENT

Using office equipment in an optimal way will make it easier for your employees to work. Place copiers and printers in easily accessible areas. Make sure the procedures and responsibilities for maintaining equipment are well known and documented so there are no unnecessary delays or confusion when something needs servicing. If no one knows who is responsible for calling the copier guy, it can delay getting things back in good working order quickly.

Office furniture is also very important to your team. Your employees sit on those chairs all day long and use those desks almost every moment they are there. A chair with a broken arm or a desk with a broken keyboard tray is a major inconvenience that can really make the workday miserable. Get broken items fixed or replaced as soon as possible.

Many times, these types of things appear gradually, so it is a good idea to assess the office furniture that your team is using yearly. These simple fixes can have a significant impact that you won't realize until the annoyances disappear.

INDIVIDUAL BOUNDARIES

Your office should have both community or shared areas, where employees use common resources like a printer, fax machine, shipping supplies, etc., and individual work areas. It's important that each employee has her own personal area and it should be clear that everyone needs to respect these boundaries. Having a space where an employee can feel at home will help her develop a personal working style and get organized in a way that benefits her responsibilities. Comfortable employees mean better productivity. If employees have items they need to share with others (files, keys, and so on), but need to keep within their personal work area, have them designate a corner or other specific location of their workspace where they will store these items. Whenever possible, this should be very visible and labeled to avoid any confusion. This will make it easy for anyone to find these items without searching through the entire desk and violating privacy.

To help ensure that people respect these boundaries, make sure everyone understands where the boundary lines are and what areas are designated as personal space. For example, Diane may have an outbox on her desk that other people take things from, but she may feel that it is part of her personal space and may not want people moving it, reorganizing it, and so on. Any violations of personal space or boundaries should be taken seriously. If it's necessary to go through an employee's personal space, you or another manager should either do it or supervise.

apples to apples A CASE STUDY

The key to the locked client file cabinet is missing and Shirley needs it immediately—it looks like an employee is going to have to go into someone's personal space to get it. The last one to have the key was Alice, but she's in the boardroom on an important conference call and cannot be interrupted. Her purse is always in the top-left drawer of her desk and Shirley believes the key is in the same drawer. Shirley comes to Paul and he watches as Alice's drawer is opened and the key is, in fact, there, along with her purse. Shirley takes the key and closes the drawer. Later, Alice insists that she had $100 in her purse and it's missing now. If Paul had not been involved, there would be a problem. But because Paul was there, he can confidently say that Shirley could not have taken the money.

RULES FOR PERSONAL ITEMS

Encourage your employees to express their individual person alities in their workspaces, within the limits set by your company. Putting up a few photos and bringing in a plant or a child's drawing can really make a dull workspace feel personal.

However, you'll need to establish some rules for appropriate decoration in the workspace. Try to define for your employees what you consider appropriate. There are some obvious no-nos—adult material, attack statements (such as "I Hate Republicans"), or gory things. You should also make it clear that items that are offensive to other employees should not be present. It's always best to err on the side of caution when it comes to items that have the potential to offend someone. Encourage employees to maintain a professional workspace at all times and remember that your employees don't have the right to complete freedom of speech in the company workplace. Outside of work, they can certainly express themselves, but they can be required to keep things professional at the office if it has an impact on the company's ability to operate effectively. Check with your HR department to see if there are any clear policies about cubicle decoration.

COMMON AREAS

Common areas tend to become disaster areas because no one feels any personal responsibility for cleaning them up. However, it's your job as a manager to stay on top of office cleanliness. Make sure there is enough space to neatly store everything that belongs in the area (creamer and sugar at a coffee area, for example). You can assign one person to a common area or you can rotate responsibility for cleaning it. If necessary, create rules about the areas, such as cleaning out the fridge once a week, picking up your scraps at a paper-cutting station, and so on. Create an atmosphere of shared responsibility for common areas. If each person cleans up after himself, the area will stay clean.

If you have a team that just won't clean up after themselves, there are a few things you can do.

- Post clear rules, such as "Please clear and wipe the table when you are through." Or "Please replace toilet paper if you use it up."
- If nothing works, create a rotating responsibility. Each person is assigned a day of the week when she must clean the room.
- If that still doesn't get the job done, explain that the use of the common area may have to be restricted or potentially eliminated. It is unlikely that you will reach this step since peer pressure will force the offending party to comply or face the consequences with the team.

Common areas are good places to post reference material, notices, and so on. Procedure or equipment manuals, company newsletters, bulletin boards with happenings (items for sale, charity golf outings, etc.) can all be placed here for general use.

MAKE THINGS FRIENDLY

Many office environments are very sterile and bland, but there are steps you can take to liven yours up. Get permission to repaint your team's area if you find it to be dingy. A few plants can make a big difference, as can framed posters. If you don't have much of a budget, encourage employees to bring in their children's art and make a large wall collage of it. Simply cleaning the inside of the windows or light coverings can really brighten an area.

Basic maintenance goes a long way toward making the workplace feel like a place that is maintained and is employee-friendly. Simple things like making sure that there is proper lighting in all areas can help ensure that employees have a pleasant experience. If light bulbs are burned out and remain so for long periods of time, it sends a message to your employees that the company doesn't care about them. Clean and functioning bathrooms are also an important component. Making sure they are stocked with tissue, towels, and soap is an absolute requirement—not a luxury.

Holiday decorations can also make a space more lively and festive. These should be sensitive to any religious or cultural diversity among your team or within your company. They also shouldn't have an impact on the team's ability to get their work done. For example, minilights strung across a cubicle wall are fine and can add a little pizzazz. However, they shouldn't be plugged into the outlet meant for the printer, forcing others to use a different printer that is farther away or not as good.

Having a positive physical environment in your office can help build your team morale, keep your good apples good, and even encourage your bad apples to adopt good work habits. Of course, the best way to solve the problem of bad apples is to avoid hiring them in the first place.

CHAPTER 13

AVOID HIRING BAD APPLES

The best way to manage bad apples is to avoid hiring them to begin with. However, with the limited amount of time you have to talk with a potential employee and observe him, you may not know how to avoid making a poor hiring choice. Knowing how to steer clear of potentially troublesome employees is an important skill and one that every manager needs to develop.

CH 12. Create a Positive Work Environment

CH 13. Avoid Hiring Bad Apples

CONCLUSION Balancing the Apple Cart

DEFINE THE JOB

The first step in finding good employees is to be very clear about what you're looking for and offering. This means you need to take some time to think about what your requirements are, what your company needs, where this position fits into your organizational chart, and how you will compensate the person you hire. Compensation should be in line with your company's wage scale. You may need to consult with your supervisor or HR manager so everyone understands what the plan is.

JOB DESCRIPTION

The job description gives potential employees a clear idea of what you need and what the position is, and gives you an opportunity to really work through what you're going to expect from this employee and what skills you need. Be as specific as possible when you do this. Instead of saying "position requires generating sales," clarify your needs and say, "the position requires the generation of thirty sales leads per month and ten closings."

If you're advertising for a new position, make sure there is no unnecessary overlap with other positions. You should also come up with a descriptive name for the position. When people read job boards or ads, they usually scan the job titles quickly. If your title does not accurately reflect the position, you may miss out on candidates who would be well suited for the job and could also get resumes from people who are not a good fit at all.

If there are other people currently in the same job at your company, understanding which ones do a good or bad job and why can be helpful information. Depending on the circumstances, they can provide a model of what to look for or warning signs of what to avoid.

DETERMINE PAY AND BENEFITS

To determine what to pay for the position, you may want to do some research. Talk to colleagues at other companies, talk with other managers in your own company, and look on sites such as Salary.com. You may need to get clearance for the salary and benefits you want to offer, so be sure to do so before posting the job.

WHERE TO FIND GOOD EMPLOYEES

The best way to ensure that you hire a good employee is to start with a good group of candidates for the position. There are several ways to find good possibilities:

- **Use contacts.** Make sure as many people as possible know that you and your company need employees. Use both your professional and personal contacts. If someone you're familiar with (a current employee, another supervisor, a colleague, your pastor) knows someone who would be a good fit for the job, you definitely want to consider him for the position.

- **Promote from within.** Post the job within your company. If you hire someone from inside, you'll be able to learn much of what there is to know about that person from the personnel file and by talking to her current manager. When people are promoted from within, there is a shorter learning curve and often a greater likelihood that the person will succeed at the new position. However, just because someone already works for your company, doesn't mean he will automatically be a good fit for this position. Interview carefully and be sure he has the necessary skills. You also want to make sure that another manager is not passing off a bad apple on you. Do careful interviews when hiring from within to learn the worth of the employee and don't just take another manager's word for it.

- **Rely on professional organizations.** Locating a legal administrator through the national legal administrator's organization (*www.alanet.org*) is a good way to ensure that you'll hear from qualified candidates. Many organizations also have job boards or newsletters listing positions that can allow you to access information about appropriate pay scales and certifications to look for in an employee.

- **Check your files.** You or your company may already have a file of resumes that were submitted for a similar position. This file contains candidates who have already expressed an interest in working for your company, so they're a good place to work from. The older the resume, the less useful it will be to you.

- **Headhunters.** Although headhunters can be very expensive, they may actually end up saving your company money. The headhunter locates potential candidates and screens them for you. You'll be presented with a roster of qualified candidates and don't have to spend weeks and months trying to locate them yourself. If the headhunter quickly finds you a candidate, you can get that employee started right away and keep your productivity up. Using a headhunter who understands your industry and has previously placed people at your company can make the process even easier.

SELECTING INTERVIEWEES

You won't want to interview everyone who applies for the job, so you need to take some time to read through the letters and resumes you've received to find the most qualified candidates. Look for people who:

- Have relevant experience
- Meet your educational criteria
- Follow instructions (by submitting what you asked for or completing forms you've requested)
- Have solid work histories

You should ideally be able to separate the resumes into three piles: definite yes, definite no, and maybe. Interview the definite yeses first.

INITIAL INTERVIEWS

Once you've located some candidates, you'll want to schedule interviews. For most positions, interviews should be a process, not a single appointment. You will probably need to see and speak to each person several times. The initial interview is the starting point from which you should be able to weed out several candidates. The importance of the position that you're hiring for will determine how in-depth the interview process should be. If you're hiring a part-time receptionist, you can probably make your decision with one interview. However, if you're hiring for a more complicated position, such as an insurance claims clerk, you may need to do at least two interviews.

INITIAL CONTACT

Whether you contact the candidate by e-mail or phone, you can get a basic first impression from these contacts. Does he respond to you within a reasonable time frame? Is she courteous and friendly? These initial contacts can help you get a feel for what the person is like and can help you gauge how serious his interest is in the job you have available.

QUESTIONS

An interview gives you an opportunity to talk to people in person and be able to understand who they really are and what they're capable of. The questions you ask are the path to gaining information about that person. The interview is guided by your questions, so it's important to choose them well.

Write your questions in advance. This ensures that you ask each candidate the same questions and allows you to gather all the important information you need. Also, taking notes throughout the interview will help you make an informed decision later on.

At the beginning of an interview you should welcome a person and encourage him to feel comfortable. You can help someone feel at ease by engaging in small talk, such as the weather, sports, current events, and so on at the start of the interview. Avoid potentially controversial topics. You should also frame how the conversation is going to go. Explain that you have thirty minutes and, if you're expecting a potential interruption (such as a phone call), let the person know. If someone else is going to participate in the meeting, let the person know that as well. Letting the job candidate know what to expect will help him feel comfortable.

Follow these tips for conducting the interview:

- **Discuss qualifications first.** Many managers like to start an interview by describing the position. This is actually a bad idea because it then allows the interviewee to tailor his description of his skills, experiences, and qualifications to meet the job description you just gave him. Instead, begin by asking questions about the person's education, experience, previous positions, and previous responsibilities.

- **Avoid yes or no questions.** You want the candidate to open up, so ask questions that require her to actually form sentences.
- **Ask for examples.** It's easy to talk in generalities, but once you ask an interviewee to give an example of a project he enjoyed or was successful at, you'll have a much clearer picture of who this person is.
- **Ask about gaps.** If there are gaps in her employment history, ask about them. If she says she was self-employed during some of these gaps, be sure to get details. Self-employment can sometimes be a veil for unemployment.

Two of the best and most revealing questions you should ask your potential employee are what he has found the most frustrating about his current job and what is the most rewarding. The answers will show how he handles situations.

apples to apples A CASE STUDY

Rosa interviewed Marcus for an editorial assistant position at a publishing house. She asked him what he found rewarding and what he found frustrating about his current job. He told her no one at his current job understood him or recognized his potential. He sounded very bitter and resentful. His attitude raised a red flag with Rosa. She further explored Marcus's attitude in a later interview, confirmed it through his references, and was able to avoid hiring him.

This example also shows that it's important to find out how the person gets along with other employees (or at least his perception of the situation). If you come right out and ask, "How do you get along with other people?" the person will probably say, "Great!" This doesn't help you. Instead, ask specific questions.

Some questions to ask include:

- Have you worked in a team environment?
- What did you like about it and what did you dislike?
- What's the biggest challenge that you find working with other people?
- Do you prefer to work with others or alone?

Listen carefully to the tone of the answers and look for facial expressions that convey annoyance.

EMPLOYMENT TESTING AND BACKGROUND CHECKS

Many companies now screen potential employees by using employment tests. These tests really are helpful (although if you've taken one you may not agree!) and can provide some reasonable insight about intelligence, personality tendencies, and skill sets. They allow you to better focus your time as an interviewer on candidates who are shown to have a better chance of being successful in the position. While personality and skill tests have been common in the workplace for some time, more and more employers are doing credit checks, background checks, and even medical tests. You need to consult with your HR manager about any testing you decide to do because of the risk of discrimination. It's illegal to use the results of these tests to discriminate based on race, color, sex, national origin, religion, disability, or age (forty or older). Use of tests and other selection procedures can also violate the federal antidiscrimination laws if they disproportionately exclude people in a particular group by race, sex, or another covered basis, unless the employer can justify the test or procedure under the law. For more information, visit *www.eeoc.gov/policy/docs/factemployment_procedures.html*.

REFERENCES

Only ask for the number of references you plan to call. If you know you only have time to call two people per candidate, don't ask for three references just because you think it sounds better. It's always a good idea to call all the references you've been given. You never know when one may offer some insight that you might not have gotten from another. When speaking with references, you'll want to start with some basic questions, such as:

- How do you know the candidate?
- How long has she worked for you or with you?
- What position did she hold?
- What are her strengths?
- What are her weaknesses?
- What would you regard as the biggest potential problem with hiring her?
- How would you describe her attitude in general?
- How would you describe her performance?
- Would you hire her if you had the opportunity?

Once you've gotten some background, tell the reference a little bit about the job the candidate has applied for and ask how he thinks she would perform in such a role. For example, if the job requires contact with vendors who may be unfriendly or difficult, ask how the reference thinks the candidate would react in that situation. If the position is a high-stress one, ask how the candidate would react to it.

Most people only list references who will give them positive reviews, and any reference that is not positive is one you should talk with in depth. Find out what the problem is and why this person is negative. If something in the interview or on the application concerned you, ask the references about it. Be aware that often a reference will tell the candidate what you asked and talked about.

Go Online for Background

Many managers Google the candidate to see if they have MySpace or Facebook pages. These pages reveal a lot about people, but keep in mind that most young people with these pages never think that a potential boss will look at them, so the pages tend to be overly candid and depict a side of the person you probably wouldn't see at the office. Websites like LinkedIn .com can also provide you with information about who the candidate knows and is associated with. Your intent should not be to snoop, but to gather as much information as possible so you can make an informed decision (which, you hope, will reduce the likelihood of hiring someone who will turn out to be a bad apple).

GUT FEELING

Many of us don't listen to our gut instincts, but when you're hiring employees, your initial instinct can be critical. If someone rubs you the wrong way when you first meet him, it's likely he will continue to do so in the future. If you have a vague feeling that there is something not quite right about the candidate, you are likely correct. Try to pinpoint what it is that's bothering you. If possible, find a way to ask the candidate some questions that will help you sort out your concerns. Don't be afraid to be direct about your concerns. It's better to address them before you hire than after.

If your initial gut feeling is a positive one, make sure you are able to back that up with the interview results and the references you call. You don't want to hire someone, find out she was a mistake, and have to tell your boss that you hired her because you simply had a good feeling about her!

BODY LANGUAGE

The way people position their bodies and move them during interviews can provide you with a wealth of nonverbal communication. Sometimes people say things with their body that they won't put into words. If you can become a reader of these signals, you'll learn a lot about the people you're interviewing.

Some warning signs include:

- **Slouching or leaning.** This type of candidate is telling you he's not fired up, excited, or interested in the position. Good candidates will sit up straight with their backs against the back of the chair.
- **No mimicking.** People who are interested in the job will unconsciously mimic your body language. If you lean forward, they will too. If you cross your legs, they will too. You can't expect candidates to play Simon Says with you, but you can look to see if there is any mimicking going on. None may be a sign of little interest. Too much mimicking can show the person is trying too hard to be what you want and may not be showing his true self.

- **Folded arms.** A potential hire who sits in front of you with her arms crossed over her chest is acting defensively and is not completely open to you or the job.
- **No hand movements.** People use their hands to talk when they feel comfortable. A job candidate who sits with his hands solidly in his lap is not displaying a lot of emotion or comfort with the interview. Also, watch out for interviewees who flap their hands around too much—this can show an overabundance of energy and lack of restraint. Drumming fingers or tapping or clicking a pen can indicate a high level of tension.
- **Lack of eye contact.** Eye contact is one of the most important parts of an interview. Someone who won't look you in the eye may be acting deceptively or may feel unprepared. Ideally, a good candidate will look at you when you are speaking. If there are other people helping you conduct the interview, the candidate should look at each person at some point during his answers to questions.

It's important to distinguish between body language that offers warnings and body language caused by simple nerves. Very few people are comfortable enough in an initial interview to act like themselves. The situation in an interview is always a charged one. If the position you're hiring for is a high-stress position, the interview should help you see how that candidate will react to stress and help you get a feel for the type of behavior you should expect. In most other cases though, you have to take the interview behavior with a grain of salt and realize that nerves may be the cause of some minor problems. You may be able to get a better look at the candidate's true personality in subsequent interviews where he should begin to feel more comfortable.

LOOK FOR PATTERNS

Patterns of behavior are the root of problems with bad employees. When you're interviewing people, keep an eye out for any patterns. Someone who is late for two interviews is likely to be an employee who can't get to work on time. An interviewee who is unfriendly on the phone with you each time you call may be someone who does not have good phone skills. Someone who always interrupts you when you are talking may be a potential problem as well.

You also need to look for patterns in the person's history, such as short stays at jobs, lack of upward mobility at a company (no career advancement or promotions), or frequent geographic relocation. Always ask about patterns like those if you identify them. They may not always signify a problem, but you don't want to dismiss them without getting an explanation.

Another pattern to look for is patterns of behavior. If you interview a woman who laughs inappropriately at some point during the interview, you can probably write it off to nerves. But if she continues to laugh inappropriately several times during both interviews you have with her, there may be a potential problem.

GET INPUT

While you'll make the hiring decision based mostly on your own impressions, it can be helpful to get input from other members of your company. Others may be able to identify problems you didn't catch and may ask revealing questions in the interview. Having another management member provide input can make you feel comfortable that you're avoiding a bad apple hire.

OTHER MANAGERS

You may wish to ask managers who are at your level in the company, or managers above you (such as your boss) to sit in on an interview. Only do this with the final one or two candidates whom you're considering (other managers don't have time to sit in on six different interviews with you). Give the other manager the basic information about the interviewee and why you think he might be a good hire, but point out your concerns as well. Remember, it's always a good idea to put the candidate at ease by letting them know that someone else will be stopping in.

Another manager can sometimes stop into an interview and play the "bad cop." If you have a few concerns about the interviewee, the other manager can come into the room and zero in on those only. After he leaves, you can play the "good cop" and possibly get some more information from the interviewee because she feels more comfortable with you. This is also sometimes a good way to see how the person will react to a challenging situation.

OTHER TEAM MEMBERS

It may seem odd to include other team members in the interview, but if your team works closely together, it can be helpful to see how your current people interact with the person you want to hire. Your employees may also ask questions you hadn't thought of that relate directly to the work process and can evaluate what kind of team cooperation will be possible with this new person.

Before setting up such an interview, talk with the team members you're asking to participate. Make it clear that you're not giving them the power to make the decision about the hire, but are interested in their input. Talk about what types of questions may be appropriate for them to ask and give them some information about the person being interviewed beforehand.

Unless you have a very small team (two or three people), it's not a good idea to invite your entire team to sit in. Not only is it intimidating for the job candidate, but it can make it difficult to have a good conversation.

Between a Rock and a Hard Place

Sometimes, no matter how carefully you interview a person and talk with references, you may still end up with a bad apple, which will quickly become evident. If you find that you have a new hire who isn't working out at all, the first thing to do is talk to the employee. Maybe her job responsibilities or your expectations were miscommunicated. Point out your concerns and give her a chance to make it right. A week is an adequate amount of time to see some change. If nothing changes, getting rid of the person is a good idea. Check with your HR department to find out what your company rules are about probationary periods (often thirty days). You may consider keeping her around until you can find someone new if she's not having a negative impact on the company.

Sometimes it can be beneficial to allow your team members to talk to the potential hire without you in the room. This meeting can give the candidate a chance to ask your team questions that will help her decide if this is a place she really wants to work, making it beneficial for everyone involved. For this to work, you must really trust your team and feel confident that they can talk with the person in a professional manner. You should set up this interview with the understanding that your employees will report back to you about the meeting.

MAKING THE CHOICE

Many times it will be evident whom you should hire, but other times it may not be so clear. If you're comparing candidates, you may want to give weight to:

- Experience working in your industry
- Experience in a similar job
- Ability to benefit the company (through contacts, client list, etc.)
- A pleasant personality
- A go-getter attitude

Some managers are tempted to hire people they see as a challenge, but this is usually a mistake because challenging people can turn out to be bad apples who cannot be turned around.

apples to apples A CASE STUDY

Ric was hiring an assistant and had two strong candidates. JoJo was more experienced, but Ric didn't think she would stay in the position long, so he hired Kenya, who had almost no experience. Ric really believed that he could teach her the ropes and he would get a lot of credit for taking a diamond in the rough and making it shine. Kenya ended up being a disaster—she never really understood the work that was required and wasn't motivated to figure it out. She was lazy and manipulative. Ric ended up being completely wrong about her, determined she was a bad apple, and had to let her go. She was too much of a challenge and couldn't be turned around.

GETTING OFF ON THE RIGHT FOOT

Once you've made the decision to hire a new employee, it's crucial that you get her off to a good start at your company. Have a plan for the kind of training or work you want her to do the first few days because the way the job starts will deeply influence her opinion and attitude toward it. Always be sure that you're there the day the person starts and personally introduce her to coworkers and other important people in the company. It can be helpful to choose another team member to be her "buddy" for the first day—a person who can answer her questions, help her with problems, and be friendly.

It's very important that you act like your true managerial self when your new employee starts. It can be tempting to be overly nice and excessively laidback, because, after all, she's just getting started. However, while you don't want to seem harsh, you also don't want to make things too easy. She needs to know what's expected of her so that there isn't disillusionment after you've invested time and money in her.

CONCLUSION

BALANCING THE APPLE CART

Bad apple employees are going to exist even in the best companies. No environment, industry, or business is immune. The challenge for you as a manager is to not let this stand in your way of building a successful team that continues to improve. When faced with this potential obstacle, you have a choice: allow bad apples to derail and distract you from your core responsibilities or use the situation to further demonstrate and grow your skills. Bad apple employees allow you to become a better manager, while continuing to create a productive and energetic work environment for everyone you supervise.

CH 12. Create a Positive Work Environment

CH 13. Avoid Hiring Bad Apples

CONCLUSION Balancing the Apple Cart

While learning the different approaches and tactics to dealing with bad apples is important, perhaps the most crucial strategy is to manage yourself. Ultimately, you have control over what you do and the decisions that you make. You set the course for your employees so it's important to lead by example. If you are disciplined enough to react to difficult situations in productive ways, you will find that bad apples are not as significant as they first appear. These situations can be viewed as opportunities to gain respect from your good apples as well.

Be prepared. It will be frustrating. There will be times when you will question if you are doing the right thing, but you shouldn't give up. Perseverance and focus are useful tools that will keep you on the right track. Keep working at it and use the ideas presented here as a guide. You will see that what works in one situation may not work in another, but focus on your goals and ensure that your actions support them at all times. Look for the successes along the way to help keep you motivated.

Remember: What separates good managers from bad is not how they act when things are going smoothly, but rather how they respond to difficult situations. Make a difference today!

ABOUT THE AUTHOR

TERRENCE SEMBER

Terrence Sember is vice president of Internet and technology services for Chakra Communications (*www.ChakraCentral.com*). He holds a BA and MBA and has worked in the Internet and technology field for more than ten years and has previous experience in other fields. He is coauthor of *The Essential Supervisor's Handbook* (Career Press, 2007). He is a member of InfoTech Niagara, the trade association of Western New York's information technology industry, with more than 6,000 members, and the Buffalo Niagara Partnership, made up of 2,500 member businesses with a quarter of a million employees. He is a member of the worldwide organization, American Management Association, with more than 700,000 members.

ABOUT THE AUTHOR

BRETTE McWHORTER SEMBER

Brette McWhorter Sember is a former attorney and author of more than thirty titles, including *The Essential Supervisor's Handbook* (Career Press, 2007) and *Project Management Strategy* (Amacom, 2008), *The Complete Credit Repair Kit* (Sourcebooks, 2004), and *The Divorce Organizer & Planner* (McGraw-Hill, 2004). Her freelance work has appeared in more than 150 publications, including *Home Business Journal* and the *New York Law Journal*, as well as many national women's, parenting, and pregnancy magazines. She is a member of ASJA. She is an expert for Clubmom .com, BabyCenter.com, ePregnancy.com, LifeTips.com, and WomansDivorce.com. Her website is *www.BretteSember.com*.

ABOUT THE FOREWORD WRITER

ROSANNE T. DEE

Rosanne T. Dee (Foreword) is principal and owner of RT Dee and Associates, a consulting firm that specializes in helping clients create people and business solutions to win in the marketplace. She focuses on the assessment of organizational culture and helping clients create the vision, values, strategies, policies, and practices that align and lead to organizational and individual success.

She has more than twenty-five years of management experience, including ten years as a senior human resource manager for a fast-growth manufacturing company. She has designed and implemented policies and procedures for a wide variety of clients, ranging from a multimillion-dollar medical products manufacturer, start-up organizations to numerous service and manufacturing organizations throughout North America.

Rosanne's professional affiliations include Fisher-Price, General Mills, Praxair, Unicell, and North American Health Plans.

INDEX

A

Advancement, 101-2
Annoying vs. bad behavior, 11-14

B

Background checks, 214-15
  online, 216
Backstabber, 22-23
Bad apples
  balance with good employees,
    107-8
  consequences of firing, 164-67
  decisions that consider, 113
  defined, 3-7
  discipline of, 149-58
  effect on good employees, 92-97
  in groups, 99
  identifying, 10-11
  and liability, 176
  and productivity, 94
  reasons for behavior, 7-9
  response to, 95-97
  rewards for, 102-3
  as scapegoats, 99-100
  signs that influence is spread-
    ing, 94-95
  steps to manage, 98

talking about, 97-100
and technology, 107
tools for working with, 104-6
types, 19-40
value of, 97-98
Behavior, 4-5, 12
Bias, 15, 27
Billable hours, 5
Body language and hiring, 217-18
Bottom line, 5
Boundaries, 202-3
Bully, 32-33

C

Career climber, 37-38
Chain of command, 60
Combatants, 30-31
Common areas, 204
Communication channels, 110-12
Company policies, 176
Conflict resolution skills, 133-48
  avoiding escalation, 140-42
  bringing parties together, 136-
    38
  common ground, 143-44
  failure, 146-48
  follow through, 146

Conflict resolution skills—*continued*
   format, 138-39
   ground rules, 139
   impact on team, 146
   implementation, 145
   interteam, 136
   'I' statements, 141
   managing yourself, 144
   neutrality, 137
   reasons for, 134-35
   resolution pathway identification, 144-45
   root of conflict determination, 142-43
Conflicts between teams, 127-32
   job responsibility reallocation, 130-31
   management conflict, 127-28
   organizational restructuring, 131-32
   physical restructuring, 129-30
   sensitivity training, 132
   solutions, 128-32
Confrontation, avoiding, 82
Consequences, 77-78
Conversation with employees
   about problems, 80-84
   effective conversation tips, 81-84
   responses, 83-84
   words that work, 84
Corporate culture, 67-69
Crisis, 38-39
Criticism, 79
   balance with praise, 103
   constructive, 151-52
   versus discipline, 150
Crying, 121

D

Defensiveness, 92, 94
Defusing situations, 196-97
Discipline, 149-58
   appropriateness of, 152
   constructive criticism, 151-52
   dealing with your feeling, 156-57
   defined, 150
   documentation of, 158
   empty threats, 154
   fallout from, 155-56
   favoritism in, 156
   how to offer, 152-55
   language for, 153-54
   privacy for, 154-55
Documentation, 11, 20, 33, 85
   of discipline, 158
   and firing, 182-83, 185
   for probation, 178-79
   for warnings, 176-78
Dress, 198
Dynamics, 47-48, 56
   interteam, 48

E

Effect on team and company of bad apples, 9
E-mail, reading employee, 161
Employee handbook, 173, 180, 181
Employees not under your supervision, 56-61
   contact with you, 56-58
   contact with your team, 58-61
   other teams, 61-63

Employment testing, 214-15
Equipment, 201
Exit interview, 169
Expectation setting, 193-95
Eye contact, 218

F

Firing
    alternatives to, 52-53
    and clients, 166
    consequences of firing bad
        apples, 164-67
    deciding on, 160
    deciding when, 162
    and documentation, 182-83, 185
    exit interview, 169
    and government employees, 181
    and health insurance, 183
    how to fire someone, 167-70
    and employee's friends, 165
    and final paychecks, 168
    an inherited employee, 53
    and legalities, 180-83
    not an option, 16-18
    and other managers, 166-67
    and personal lives, 164
    and quitting, 173-74
    reasons for, 160-62
    and references, 184
    two weeks notice, 181
    and unemployment insurance,
        174, 183-85
    when not to fire, 162-63
    and your feelings, 170-73
Food, 13-14
Friendly environment, 205

G

Goals, 44-45
    individual, 45
    team, 45
Good employees
    advancement, 101-2
    attitudes, 105-6
    balance with bad apples, 107-8
    balance of criticism and praise,
        103
    communication channels for,
        110-12
    connections with, 100-1
    help for working with bad
        apples, 104-6
    effect of bad apples on, 92-97
    explaining steps to manage bad
        apples, 98
    maintaining, 100-13
    making good employees part of
        the process, 103-4
    and morale, 109-10
    response when good employee
        starts to go bad, 95-97
    rewards for, 102
    signs that bad apple influence is
        spreading, 94-95
    talking to about bad apples,
        97-100
    technology use and working
        with bad apples, 107
    tools for working with bad
        apples, 104-5
    training for, 102
    and trust and respect, 112
Gossips, 20-22

H

Headhunters, 210
Health insurance, 183
Hiring, 207-23
  background checks, 214-15,
    216
  and body language, 217-18
  choosing an employee, 222
  contacts, 209
  defining the job, 208-9
    employment gaps, 213
  employment testing, 214-15
  files, 210
  finding good employees, 209-10
  getting off on the right foot,
    223
  and gut feelings, 216-17
  headhunters, 210
  initial contact, 211-12
  initial interviews, 211
  input on, 219-21
  job description, 208
  patterns, 219
  pay and benefits, 209
  professional organizations, 230
  promotion from within, 209-10
  qualifications, 212-13
  questions to ask, 212-14
  references, 215-16
  selecting interviewees, 210-11
Hygiene, 34

I

Idea theft, 35-36
Improvement plan for employee,
  85-87
  disagreement by employee,
    86-87
  follow through, 87-88
  Incompetent, 36-37
  Inherited employees, 41-53
  background information, 42-44
  creating relationships with,
    47-49
  creating respect, 48-49
  dynamics, 47-48
  firing, 52-53
  goals, 44-45
  management of, 45-46
  strengths, 42-46
  tipping point, 50-52
  value to company, 50
  weaknesses, 42-46
Input on hiring, 219-21
  from other managers, 220
  from other team members,
    220-21
Interactions with employees,
  192-93
Interteam conflict resolution, 136

J

Job
  description, 42-43, 208
  hater, 39-40
  responsibility reallocation,
    130-31

L

Lazy bones, 29-30
Liability, 176
Liar, 28
Listening skills, 112

M

Management conflict, 127-28
Modeling good behavior, 197-99
Morale, 109-10
Motivation, 29-30, 73-89
    causation, 75-76
    consequences, 77-78
    follow through, 87-88
    in general, 88-89
    plan for improvement, 85-87
    problem identification, 74-75
    rewards, 76-77
    talking about the problem,
        80-84
    and your own feelings, 78-80
Motivational intervention, 92-93
Music, 14

N

Narcissist, 26-28
Negativity, 9
Noise control, 200-1

O

Organizational restructuring,
    131-32
Our Lady of Perpetual Crisis,
    38-39
Outsourcing, 172
Overachievers, 126-27

P

Passive-aggressive, 23-25
Performance, 5-7
Personal
    items, 203
    opinions, 14-15
Personality conflicts
    dealing with, 122-23
    and gender, 123-25
    helping the innocent party, 125
    intervention, 121-22
    between one person and others,
        125-27
    with overachievers, 126-27
    prevention of, 117
    reasons for, 116-17
    between teams, 127-32
    and two team members, 120-25
    you are involved in, 119-20
Personality trait, 12
Physical
    environment, 199-205
    restructuring, 129-30
Poisoner, 31-32
Positive feedback, 87
Praise, balance with criticism, 103

Probation, 178-79
Productivity, 5-7, 12, 13-14, 15
    effect on by bad apple, 94
Promotion from within the company, 42

Q

Quitting, 173-74

R

References, 184, 215-16
Rejection, 92, 93-94
Respect from employees, 48-49,
    112
Responsibility for hires, 16
Rewards, 76-77
    for bad apples, 102-3
    for good behavior, 102

S

Scapegoats, 99-100
Sensitivity training, 132
Silence, 83
Slob, 33-34
Small office tips to avoid conflict,
    130
Space, 199-200
Standard operating procedures, 6,
    24, 30
Strengths of employees, 42-46
    management based on, 45-46

Supervisors,
    above you, 65-67
    at your level, 64-65
Suspensions, 179
    disciplinary, 179
    nondisciplinary, 179

T

Team
    building, 195-96
    culture, 190-92
Team-to-team conflict, 61-63,
    127-32
    job responsibility reallocation,
        130-31
    management conflict, 127-28
    organizational restructuring,
        131-32
    physical restructuring, 129-30
    sensitivity training, 132
    signs of conflict, 128
    solutions, 128-29
Termination. *See* Firing
Thief, 35-36
Tipping point, 50-52, 160
Traffic flow, 200
Training for employees, 102
Trust, 112

U

Unemployment insurance, 174,
    183-85
Unreliable, 36-37

V

Value
    to company of employee, 50
    of employee to company, 16-17
    reinforcing of bad apple, 97-98

W

Warnings, 176-78
Waster, 25-26
Weaknesses of employees, 42-46
    management based on, 45-46
Whiner, 36
Work
    environment, 12
    hours, 198
    volume and quantity of, 5